James Ramsay, Samuel Beach

An Essay on the Treatment and Conversion of African Slaves in the

British Sugar Colonies

James Ramsay, Samuel Beach

An Essay on the Treatment and Conversion of African Slaves in the British Sugar Colonies

ISBN/EAN: 9783744793711

Printed in Europe, USA, Canada, Australia, Japan

Cover: Foto ©ninafisch / pixelio.de

More available books at **www.hansebooks.com**

A N

E S S A Y

ON THE

TREATMENT AND CONVERSION

OF

AFRICAN SLAVES

IN THE

BRITISH SUGAR COLONIES.

BY THE

REVEREND JAMES RAMSAY, M. A.

VICAR OF TESTON, IN KENT.

God hath made of one Blood all Nations of the Earth, for to dwell on all the Face of the Earth, Acts xvii. 26.

He that stealeth a Man, and selleth him, or if he be found in his Hand, he shall surely be put to death, Exodus xxi. 16.

———

D U B L I N:

PRINTED FOR T. WALKER, C. JENKIN, R. MARCHBANK, L. WHITE, R. BURTON, P. BYRNE.

M,DCC,LXXXIV.

THE

PREFACE.

A LETTER of an ordinary length, in anſwer to the humane one which is here ſubjoined, gave beginning to this performance. By frequent tranſcription, it ſenſibly increaſed in ſize, and extended itſelf to collateral ſubjects, till it had become ſomething like a ſyſtem for the regulation and improvement of our ſugar colonies, and the advancement and converſion of their ſlaves.

On ſubmitting the manuſcript to thoſe, who were much better judges than the author could pretend to be, of the preſent prevailing taſte (and many perſons of rank and learning have honoured it with a peruſal) the account of the treatment of ſlaves in our colonies engaged their ſympathy, and the plan for their improvement and converſion had their hearty good wiſhes. But they exhorted him, almoſt all with one voice, to ſuppreſs every part that tended to introduce thoſe political diſcuſſions,

which

which muft be unavoidable in treating of the
ftate of colonies, and their dependence on a
mother country.

. As the author had, from the firft, no private
views to gratify in the plan, and wifhed only
to give it every poffible chance of fuccefs
with the public, their decifion was final with
him ; and in conformity to it, every thing that
related to the improvement, and better government of the colonies, has been omitted. By
this alteration in the original form of the work,
it has neceffarily loft fomething of that fyftem-
atic order, which contributes fo much to the
beauty of compofitions, and leads fo plea-
fantly on from premifes to conclufion. But
humanity is its objeƈt, not reputation. When
the finer feelings of the foul are engaged, it
would be a criminal trifling to aim at amufement.

    I will not infult the reader's underftanding,
by an attempt to demonftrate it to be an objeƈt
of importance, to gain to fociety, to reafon
and religion, half a million of our kind, equally
with us adapted for advancing themfelves in
every art and fcience, that can diftinguifh man
from man, equally with us made capable of
looking forward to and enjoying futurity. I
rather wifh to call in his benevolence, his

confcience, his intereft, to give their aid in carrying on the work. The people, whofe improvement is here propofed, toil for the Britifh ftate. The public, therefore, has an intereft in their advancement in fociety. And what is here claimed for them ? Not bounties, or gifts from parliament, or people; but leave to become more ufeful to themfelves, their mafters, and the ftate. And furely a plan, that has fuch an end in view, needs only to be explained to procure a general prepoffeffion in its favour. While the man of feeling finds every generous fentiment indulged in the profpect which it opens, the politician, the felfifh, will have all their little wifhes of opulence, and accumulation fully realized. The defign then, muft have every man of every complexion combined in its behalf; and there is nothing to be accounted for but the author's courage, in prefuming to offer to the public his thoughts in particular on the fubject.

From the manner in which this work had its beginning, it will appear that neither vanity, nor felf-fufficiency, led the author to the attempt. It was not till after the feventh copy had been read, and its purpofe approved of by many perfons of worth and judgment, that he entertained the moft diftant thoughts of publication. Even now, that it has undergone every

fuggefted

fuggefted correction, and received every improvement that three tranfcriptions in fucceffion
could give it, on their opinion, rather than his
own, he refts the probability of its proving
acceptable to the public.

Not to be guilty of ftifling what had a generous purpofe in view, and poffibly might do
good, if fo it pleafed God, has been, from
the firft, as far as refpected himfelf, the only
inducement. Profit he difclaims ; and willingly
would he transfer all the credit that can poffibly
arife from it, to him who would take on him
the cenfure. Yet fhould he not forgive himfelf, were he to difcover that ill nature had
fharpened a fingle expreffion in the Effay, or
dragged an unlucky object of refentment into
view. To blame has not been a pleafant tafk.
He has fuffered more from the neceffity of doing
it, than the perfons affected will probably do
from the application ; which yet, except in
one cafe, muft be the work of confcience with
themfelves. In this cafe, the perfon who is the
object, is of fuch an happy difpofition, as to be
incapable of feeling cenfure, and of that eftablifhed character, that nothing can hurt him.
The public, therefore, has a right to him,
as to a beacon placed near a dangerous quick
fand.

To

To conclude: the reader has here the remarks of about twenty years experience in the Weſt-Indies, and above fourteen years particular application to the ſubject. If it draws the attention due to its importance, the author will have the ſatisfaction of reflecting, that he has not lived in vain for his country and mankind. And this conſideration will ſmooth before him the otherwiſe rugged paths of life. Should it fail in anſwering his well meant purpoſe, ſtill the thoughts of having made the attempt, will pleaſe on reflection; nor will the intention loſe its reward there, where his particular aim is to be found acceptable.

Letter referred to above, which ſuggeſted to the Author the Conſideration of the following Subject.

I will omit any apology, however needful, for offering my thoughts on the ſubject of ſlavery, to one, whoſe office and opportunities among ſlaves muſt induce him to think and act what is right reſpecting them. The moſt I can hope for is, to echo to him ſome of his own reflections, which perhaps the univerſal careleſſneſs and indifference prevailing in every thing that concerns them, may, at times, cauſe him to paſs inattentively by, or conſider leſs than their importance deſerves.

I am

I am fure Mr. —— muft always think himfelf not only obliged to ufe his flaves with
kindnefs, but alfo viewing them as fellow-
creatures, bound to extend his care to the
fecurity of their eternal happinefs, by inftructing them in the relation which they bear to the
great Author of their being, and gracious Redeemer of their fouls, and in the duty arifing
from that relation, as it is revealed in the
gofpel, and is required of all men, who feek
after future happinefs. A care which, however
contrary to the ufual policy of mafters, would
be the moft probable means of making flaves
diligent and faithful ; for it would awaken
confcience within them, to be a ftrict overfeer,
and a fevere monitor, whom they could not
evade. This is a confequence, that if duly
confidered, might induce even thofe who, neglecting to take Providence into the account,
confider only how they fhall make the moft of
their ftock, to afford their flaves opportunities
of learning their duty; allowing them, for example, fome portion of the week for procuring
their fubfiftence, and fetting the Lord's day
apart for religious inftruction.

Still granting that mafters, who look no
farther than prefent profit, may laugh at the
far-fetched expectation, furely men who believe
in revelation cannot indulge a doubt but that
the

the treating of them like fellow-creatures, and
the fhewing of mercy to their fouls, will on
the whole more advance the mafter's real intereft, than a method which fuffers them to
continue in brutifh ignorance of themfelves and
their Creator; which obliges them to labour
for the fupport of their bodies, on a day fet
apart for the improvement of their fouls.

I know in this cafe it is argued, " to fuppofe
" that the work of five days may poffibly be
" found as profitable to owners, as that of fix
" days, is to expect that God will work a
" miracle to reward the indulgence; an ex-
" traordinary exertion of power, which on fo
" trivial an occafion, it would be prefumptuous
" to look for." But when in any fituation,
we doubt God's juftice or goodnefs, we injure
his power and wifdom, for thefe act under
their influence. And when we imagine him
refting at a diftance, or acting only in great
events, we entertain improper notions of his
relation to the work of his own hands. Scrip-
ture and reafon, when they contemplate the
Divine nature, join to reprefent him as ever
prefent to all his works, as quickening every
thing that liveth, upholding whatever hath a
being, as directing the operations of nature, and
guiding the actions of men, all to their proper
purpofes, in a manner indeed that we cannot
compre-

comprehend ; but fo, that a fparrow falls not to the ground without his permiffion, and that a cup of cold water given for his fake, doth not efcape his notice, nor go without its reward ; yet in a manner, which leaves unreftrained that liberty, by which moral agents become accountable for their actions. And if this be the ftate of things, under God's government, can we doubt of *their* recompenfe, who, in conformity to God's injunctions laid on our firft parents, and fince often renewed, allow themfelves and their dependents leifure, on the Lord's day, to learn their Creator's will, and pay him a rational homage and duty ? Humbly to believe and expect this, as declared to us in God's general promifes in fcripture, is an inftance of faith that we cannot refufe to his veracity, who has engaged to perform it.

Even were we unable to conceive a particular method, by which a compenfation for this relinquifhed part of our fervants labour could be effected, when we on that account conclude, that the obedience will reflect no benefit on us, we diftruft God's promifes, or doubt of his ability to find a way to reward our compliance with his will. And yet, without working a manifeft miracle, God may give fuccefs to our endeavours, in a thoufand ways, which fhall feem to be the natural effects of induftry, or that

unknown

unknown direction of human affairs, which in
common account is called chance. He may
make us fkilful in managing occafions, fagacious
in forefeeing events. He may preferve us from
expenfive illnefs, guard us from mifchievous neighbours. He may blefs us with faithful fervants.
He may incline mens affections to us, and make
them inftruments in promoting our profperity.
Endlefs are the methods by which, in an unper-
ceived manner, he can turn the common accidents of life to reward men who prefer duty to
prefent advantage, who co-operate with his
benevolence in promoting the happinefs of their
fellow-creatures.

To doubt of a reward, even in this world,
whenever it fhall be, on the whole, beft for us,
is to doubt of the propriety and efficacy of
prayer, and to cut off our hopes of its fuccefs.
Yet God invites us to make our requefts known
unto him, and folemnly promifes, that when we
afk we fhall receive. That it will be fo, even
in this life, we may pofitively conclude, if we
confider only the confequence of this juft reflection, " What is called the ordinary courfe of
" Providence, which governs events, is not the
" effect of blind chance, of uncontroulable
" fate, but a wife and orderly chain of caufes and
" effects, adapted by the Almighty contriver,
" as nicely to the conduct of free agents, as
" to

" to the inftinΔs of brutes, or the laws of vege-
" table and inanimate matter."

It is owned even by men who confider flaves
as property, and who, having bought them,
conclude that they have a right to make the
moft of their money, that the working of flaves
beyond their ability, fhortens their lives, and
checks their population. Do not fuch men acknowledge in this, ftrong traces of Divine juftice,
punifhing cruelty and thirft of gain by the moft
natural means, by making them counteraΔ and
defeat their own purpofe. And by parity of
reafoning may we not expeΔ Providence to
profper by means as natural, our humane, benevolent attention to wretches, whom the crimes
and avarice of felfifh men have placed in our
power ? With refpeΔ to religion, unlefs we
deny revelation to be a blefling, or benefit to
mankind, we cannot hold ourfelves blamelefs,
if we forbear ufing our beft endeavours to communicate the knowledge of it to every one within our reach. And whatever may be our fuccefs
in other refpeΔs, the pains that we ufe to improve the minds of our fellow creatures, will
return with advantage into our own bofoms.
God's grace will be ftirred up within us, and
our own difpofition and behaviour will be
correΔed and amended.

Introduc-

Introductory Address, in Answer to the preceding Letter.

I have perufed with attention, your humane and pious remarks on the treatment of flaves in the Britifh colonies. I think myfelf honoured by your fuppofing me, in particular, capable of being influenced in my behaviour towards them, by a confideration fo benevolent, as a refpect to their moral improvement, and their eternal welfare. In return, allow me to think highly of the heart, that with a good will, in which the meaneft and moft diftant of your kind have a fhare, can, in the caufe of humanity and religion, thus warmly intereft you for fuch unpitied, and defpifed objects as our flaves in general are.

An account which may be depended on, in a matter wherein humanity is nearly concerned, cannot be unfatisfactory to a mind, turned like yours to all the tender feelings. And though I fear the emotions which this account muft naturally raife in your breaft, will not be of the cheerful kind, yet I doubt not of its producing reflections, which you would not willingly have been without. An humble refignation to the meafures of Providence, is our duty at all times ; but then efpecially, when our concern for God's glory, and our brother's eternal welfare, feems to mark out an object of our wifhes

and

and prayers, which God is pleafed to keep
referved among the hidden things of his government, till his own good time fhall come to
reveal, and give it to the world.

I wifh indeed, for your eafe, that I could
have comprehended any tolerable view of the
fubject, within more moderate limits; but it
became complex under my hands, and drew after
it a variety of confiderations. Happy ftill fhould
I have thought myfelf, could I have made
this view, fuch as it is, exprefs what you
charitably wifh it might unfold; could I inform
you, that we are careful of the bodies, and tender
of the fouls of thefe our fellow-creatures, thus
fubmitted to our power, thus abandoned to our
humanity. But truth requires a different, a
mournful tale of unconcern and unfeeling neglect.

To make this view more complete, I fhall
firft confider the feveral natural and artificial
ranks that take place in focial life, and more
particularly that of mafter and flave in the
European colonies. I fhall fhew how much
the public will be profited, and how much the
mafter would gain, by advancing flaves in focial life. I fhall fhew how this advancement in
fociety, and their improvement in religion, muft
neceffarily go hand in hand, and affift each
other, if either one, or both thefe purpofes, be
our view refpecting them. As extravagance
and

and avarice have begun of late to make fad encroachments on that reft of the fabbath, which
hitherto had been reckoned facred ; in addition
to your pious reafons for fetting it apart for
the purpofes of religion; I fhall prove how
much this inconfiderate robbery hurts the mafter's own intereft.   I fhall affert the claim of
the Negroes to attention from us, by explaining
their natural capacity, and proving them to be
on a footing of equality in refpect of the reception of mental improvement, with the natives of any other country.   And in conclufion
I fhall lay down a plan for their improvement,
and converfion.

CONTENTS.

C O N T E N T S.

CHAP. II.

CHAP. II. THE ADVANCEMENT OF SLAVES WOULD AUGMENT THEIR SOCIAL IMPORTANCE.   Page 88

CHAP. III. THE ADVANCEMENT OF SLAVES MUST ACCOMPANY THEIR RELIGIOUS INSTRUCTION.   Page 129

E S S A Y

ON THE

TREATMENT AND CONVERSION

OF

AFRICAN SLAVES

IN THE

BRITISH SUGAR COLONIES.

CHAP. I.

Of the various Ranks in Social Life.

THERE is a natural inequality, or diverſity, which prevails among men that fits them for ſociety, enables them to fill up all the different offices of poliſhed life, and forms their varied abilities, nay, even their particular defects and wants, into a firm band of union. Where the arrangement of theſe varied attributes in man is conducted in ſociety by the views of nature, or the dictates of revelation which explain and inforce them, there the feel-

B   ings

ings and interefts of the weaker, or inferior
members, are confulted equally with thofe of
the ftronger or fuperior. Each man takes that
ftation for which nature intended him ; and his
rights are fenced around, and his claims are
reftrained, by laws prefcribed by the Author of
nature: for He is the only ·rightful legiflator;
and human regulations are in a moral fenfe
binding, only when they can be traced immediately, or in principle, to this pure origin. As
the creation of man had the general improvement and happinefs of the race in view, every
law that refpects him muft fuppofe an attention
to this purpofe of his being, and therefore cannot regard the intereft of one at the expence of
another. All, as far as is confiftent with general
good, muft be left to the free ufe of their
powers and acquifitions, or of life, liberty, and
property. In the ufe of thefe, within the limits
of law, confifts the only equality that can take
place among men ; and it is evident that the
extent of this ufe muft vary according to the
different fituation of each individual, and the
capacity, or power of exertion, which he
poffeffeth, and farther muft be affected by the
ftate of improvement, that the community, of
which he is a member, has attained.

Oppofed to this law of nature, and of God,
that gives and fecures to every man the rights
adapted to his particular ftation in fociety, ftands

the

the artificial, or unnatural relation of mafter
and flave; where power conftitutes right;
where, according to the degree of his capacity
of coercion, every man becomes his own legiflator, and erects his intereft, or his caprice,
into a law for regulating his conduct to his
neighbour. And as the one draws its origin
from the heavenly fountain of benevolence, fo
the other may be traced to the infernal enemy
of all goodnefs. For here no mutual benefit is
confulted, but every wifh, every feeling, is fubmitted to the mandate of a felfifh tyrant. Yet
the influence of this luft for acting the mafter
has been fo univerfal, and has obtained fo long,
as to oblige us alfo, in principle, to deduce it
immediately from that love of power, which,
within the boundaries prefcribed by nature,
makes a part of our conftitution; it not being
poffible to account for its having fo generally
prevailed, as we find it has in the world, on
any other fuppofition than its being an abufe of
what is natural to mankind, excited and che-
rifhed in them by an enemy to their virtue and
happinefs.

For, as far back as hiftory carries us, we
read of mafter and flave. Even in the favage
ftate, cuftom, which leaves men on a footing of
equality, has enflaved wives. Among our
negro flaves, he who cannot attach to himfelf
a wife, or fubdue any other creature, buys

B 2   fome

some half starved dog, over whom he may exercise his tyrannic disposition. If these be the unalienable claims of human nature; and this the practice of mankind opposed to them, how necessary must it be to fix such boundaries, as may preserve the rights of the weak from the incroachments of the strong. And this cannot be done in a more effectual manner, than by drawing the natural, and the artificial state of society, each in its proper colours, and leaving the decision to the common sense of mankind.

S E C T. I.

The Ranks into which the Members of a Community necessarily separate.

IN every independent state, whether monarchy or republic, that has got beyond the first steps of civilization, the people, or citizens, naturally divide into sovereign and subject, master and family, employer and employed; all other ranks being arbitrary or artificial.

The sovereign declares and executes the will of the people at large. He must therefore be supreme, or uncontroulable by any particular number, or part of the people. His authority must extend over all ranks, comprehend all possible cases, and conclude every particular district. In this sense he is arbitrary, or intrusted

trufted with the power of enacting and abro-
gating laws, within the limits which man's conftitution, and the dictates of morality prefcribe.
But as the fovereign, whether hereditary or
elective, permanent or temporary, one or many
acting together in one body, is intrufted with
this power for the benefit of the people, which
fuppofeth it to be exercifed for the general
good ; therefore the law, or will of the fovereign, fhould be declared in general terms, that
it may affect individuals only by inference in
particular cafes, and conclude the perfon of the
fovereign in his ordinary conduct, and individual capacity, equally with the fubject.*

It is the general purpofe of every government, that, in extraordinary cafes, conftitutes
the people judges of their fovereign's conduct,
and juftifies them in refuming a power, which
in

---

* This circumftance is carried to a great length in the
Britifh conftitution with the happieft effects. The Houfe of
Peers helps to compofe the legiflature ; but each member, as
an individual, continues fubject to the laws. The Houfe of
Commons poffeffes, for a time limited, a fhare in the legif-
lation ; but each reprefentative is a private citizen, under the
operation of the laws ; and, after a time, the whole mixes
with the mafs of the people, to obey, as fubjects, thofe fta-
tutes that they had affifted to frame. The perfon of the king
alone, out of refpect to his office, is not made the object of
coercive law. It is this mixed character of legiflator and
citizen in our rulers that makes authority compatible with
freedom ; not the particular proportion of thofe who have the
privilege of electing them, or their numbers, or the period
for which they may have been chofen.

in refpect of its end, muft be confidered as delegated. Such a cafe happened at the revolution. But the occafion may fafely continue to
be left, as it was then, to the feelings of the
people. Defigning men, otherwife unable to
work themfelves into notice, are, under the
mafk of patriotifm, fo ready to fet up, at every
trifle, a clamour againft government, to enhance
their price, or pave the way to their own ambition, that a virtuous citizen will not eafily
fuffer himfelf to be drawn in to join the cry.

A free ftate, then, is that in which known
laws bind equally fovereign and fubject. A
proclamation forbidding the exportation of grain
is an act of power, refting on the propriety of
the meafure. A vote of credit is as illegal a
manner of raifing money on the fubject, as was
formerly fhip-money, or a benevolence; though
it may not be followed by all their bad confequences. Both fhew a defect in the conftitution, which wants to be corrected by a general
law, prefcribing the proper conduct in particular
exigencies. The law that fhut up Bofton Port
was hard, becaufe particular. A law to fhut
up every port, where the revenue laws are re-
fifted, would be juft and equitable. Thus
might a dictatorial authority, (I mean a latent
power to be occafionally called forth) which is
neceffary in every ftate, be eftablifhed on a legal
foundation,

foundation, and be kept from tranfgrefling its
due bounds. *

Families are, in the detail, what communities are at large, except that the head, or
mafter of the family, having a kind of property, either continued or temporary, in all
under his roof, governs by the dictates of difcretion, rather than by known laws. Still the
good, even of the loweft member of the family,
muft be a co-operating principle. And that
family, whofe government approaches neareft
to the regular method, which prefcribed known
rules fuppofe, where the claims, and duty, or
bufinefs, of each individual is diftinctly afcertained, will, on the whole, be beft managed,
and allow the perfons compofing it to enjoy the
greateft poffible freedom in their ftations.

In

* The cafes, for which it is neceffary to provide a dictatorial power, may eafily be forefeen, and be provided for in
one general ftatute, to be binding till the legiflature can be
affembled to deliberate on the fubject. The circumftances that
make it proper to fufpend the Habeas Corpus Act, to open or
fhut the ports, to lay embargoes, to give a vote of credit,
may eafily be enumerated. But arbitrary undefined power
has charms too alluring to be refigned by any, who find themfelves in poffeffion of it. Even our Houfe of Commons,
while acting as guardian of the privileges of the people,
choofes to fubmit its right of commitment, in cafes of contempt, to the capricious decifion of any ordinary magiftrate,
rather than permit the circumftances of the claim to be defined by a pofitive law.

In this light the rank of master and servant is comprehended in that of family; servants, as a part of the family, are subject to its rules, and, as contributing to its ease, are intitled to its advantages. But as the agreement between the master and servant is voluntary, prescribing the duty on one side, and ascertaining the wages on the other, it may likewise be considered under the head of employer and employed. The want, at first view, appears to be reciprocal; but custom has universally affixed to property the idea of superiority over personal ability, or labour. It is in this particular view, of emolument of office, that magistrates may be said to be the servants of the people, though when their authority, and not their maintenance, is considered, they may be said to partake of sovereignty.

The possessing of materials, or a subject to be improved for use by the skill or labour of another, supposeth in the possessor a right to prescribe the manner in which that skill is to be exercised, or that labour performed; and on allowing a certain reward or advantage to the man, thus employed, to appropriate to his (the possessor's) own use the labour, or improved materials. This superiority is balanced on the side of the workman, by his being free to refuse or accept the condition. It varies with the demand for labour, and with the number
of

of thofe, who offer themfelves to the work; but mutual want and mutual utility is the band that conneds them togetħer.

Similar to this, is the relation between the mechanic, or artizan, and his cuftomer. The artizan provides his own materials, and works for public: yet, though he fets his own price on his workmanfhip; and the cuftomer, without having made a previous bargain, can only refufe or agree to the condition, the confideration of having given occafion for the employment, in moft cafes, transfers the fuperiority to the cuftomer.

In the cafe of the learned profeffions, there is, indeed, fome variety; but the like analogy of employment on the one fide, and encouragement on the ~ other, runs through the whole. Particular perfons ftudy, and make themfelves acquainted with fciences, that are generally ufeful, with a view of being employed by the public, and of drawing a maintenance, and deriving diftin6tion from the exercife of their feveral profeffions.

Religion, independent of its relation to the Supreme Being, is fo neceffary to fupply the defe6t of law, and to inforce obedience to government by the influence of confcience, that hitherto, in every polifhed ftate, it has made a part of the conftitution; and becaufe it

B 5 · is

is apt to be perverted to bad purpofes, by ill
defigning men, its profeffors have always been
an important object of the public attention.*
They are fettled in every little corner of the ftate
as monitors, or cenfors of the people, and they
have their maintenance afcertained out of the
labours of thofe, whom they are appointed to
exhort and inftruct. Their fupport cannot,
any more than that of the magiftrates, be left
by government to the voluntary choice of the
people, becaufe thofe, who moft need to be
controuled by the miniftry of both, favour their
inftitution leaft, and would be far from contributing willingly to their maintenance. It
would be unjuft to expect, that the good citizen
fhould alone be taxed to fupport that magiftrate,
whom the conduct of the bad renders efpecially
neceffary; or that the pious man alone fhould
contribute to maintain that minifter, who, as
far as refpects the ftate, is eftablifhed chiefly to
moderate the profligacy of the vicious. The
loweft members of the ftate, men infenfible of
the neceffity of eftablifhments, and generally
unable

---

* If it be objected, that the original conftitution of feveral
of the American provinces is an exception; it may be anfwered,
that thefe provinces were fettled under the protection of a
ftate, of whofe conftitution an eftablifhed religion made an
effential part; and, at a period, when the hopes and fears of
futurity had a general influence, independent of public eftablifhments; and that they have not had a length of time, or,
till within thefe few laft years, been in circumftances to fhew
the genuine effects of fuch a peculiarity.

unable to contribute to them, yet at the fame time objects of them, and poffeffing importance fufficient to demand the public care, are the great confideration in the inftitution of magiftrate and minifter. The public, therefore, muft eftablifh equally, and maintain both. The clergy, by their eftablifhment, become fervants of the public, for promoting order and good conduct among the people, by the hopes and fears of religion. As fuch they have their duty prefcribed, and their maintenance, and rights, afcertained by law; which fixes the limits of each, and prevents their encroachments.

Men are fo attentive to whatever regards their health, or property; and the emoluments, and diftinction, which accompany eminence in the profeffions relating to them, encourage fuch numbers to apply to them, that government has feldom been obliged to meddle with the practice of law or phyfic. A man applies to that phyfician, or lawyer, who has his confidence; and he muft exert fkill and addrefs to preferve that diftinction. Here the dependence and utility are reciprocal, and adequate to the purpofe. Thefe profeffions, though a confequence of fociety, yet refpect each man chiefly as an individual; on this account, except in flagrant abufes, they are fafely left to private intereft; and private exertion. But religion, in its eftablifhment,

refpecting

refpecting chiefly public order, and private improvement only as far as it is fubfidiary to the other, its profeffors are confidered as auxiliaries to the magiftrate, and thus, being fervants of the ftate, are fupported at the public charge.

In the profeffion of arms there is fomething more particular; but ftill the general analogy takes place. In it one part of the community comes under certain engagements for the prefervation of the whole; but the exigency is supposed to be preffing, and the purpofe national. When it is neceffary to eftablifh an army, the foldier becomes obliged to obey his general. Here the foldier protects himfelf, his family, his country: and to do this with effect, he fubmits to fuch orders as are conducive to that end; and in the exercife of his duty his country cares for, and maintains, him. He, therefore, is alfo the fervant of the public, and, as fuch, is employed, and maintained by it; being as neceffary, in time of peace, to preferve the little police that licentioufnefs has fuffered to remain among us, as, in time of war, to defend us from our enemies.

Now in the cafe of the laws, which refpect government and people, the rule is general, fixed, and known, and equally binds the fovereign and citizen. Prejudice, caprice, or intereft, cannot fingle out an individual to
tyrannize

tyrannize over him. In the cafe of a family, its ftrict union and affection bind it in one common intereft, and caufe the members to rejoice or fuffer together. In the cafe of the labourer or artizan, he being at liberty to accept or refufe an offer from a particular employer or cuftomer, and this laft being alfo free in making his agreement, and obliged to comply with it, when determined on; thefe conditions fecure both parties equally from injury and oppreffion. In the learned profef-fions, the like circumftances produce fimilar effects. Even in the profeffion of arms an equa-lity is preferved in the compact, and fentiment and honours compenfate for the refignation of fome of the privileges of citizenfhip.

But in the arbitrary relation of mafter and flave, no law reftrains the one, no election or compact fecures the other. The mafter may invade the deareft rights of humanity, and trample on the plaineft rules of juftice; the flave cannot change his tyrant, or remonftrate againft the impropriety, perhaps impoffibility, of his tafk.

The authority which men allow to the laws that govern them, has its foundation in general utility, and the reafon of things : and as all law is, or ought to be founded on our conftitution, it, according to what has been obferved, draws its
ultimate

ultimate fanction from the God of nature, and
thus interefts confcience in the obedience due
to it. Here the equality and comprehenfivenefs
of the rule fecure the individual from oppreffion ;
he can be affected only together with the community, or when he puts himfelf in the cafe
forbidden generally by the law. Hence it is
that all Bills of Attainder muft carry oppreffion
and injuftice in their very form, being calculated
not for general utility or prevention, as laws
fhould be, but for particular deftruction; not
for guarding againft crimes, but for creating
them. The deference claimed by the employer
or cuftomer, and the refpect paid by, or to the
learned profeffions, according to the rank of the
perfons concerned, have their foundation in the
regard fhewn to wealth, learning, or power;
and their excefs is guarded againft by the nature
of the compact, and the power of affent lodged
with the labourer, artizan, or inferior perfon.
Now as far as the deference refpecting the
employer extends, it fuppofeth as real a fuperiority, limited only in its operation to the
defign thereof, as that of mafter over flave; and
as it arifeth from the ranks into which fociety
univerfally feparates men, it may be called focial
fervitude, which muft take place in the freeft
ftate.*

Here

* In the conteft between Britain and America, it may be
remarked, that the friends of the latter contended not for the
equality

Here the fervant makes his compact with the
mafter, or fuperior, and frames it to agree
with his feelings, and to fall in with his
abilities; and when the terms of his agreement
are fulfilled, his time and his enjoyments are in
his own power. But in the flavery of our
colonies, the larger part of the community is
literally facrificed to the lefs; their time, their
feelings, their perfons, are fubject to the intereft,
the caprice, the fpite of mafters and their fubftitutes, without remedy, without recompence,
without profpects. This may be called artificial fervitude, unprofitable to the public, burdenfome even to the mafter, intolerable to the
fervant, repugnant to humanity.

A law, for the purpofe of police, may direct
the ftrength and induftry of the citizens to a
particular object; as when it encourages, by a
temporary

equality of men, confidered as individuals unconnected in
fociety, till mutual benefit brought them together, and formed
the diftinction of ranks; for. in this light Americans have
made as inconfiderate mafters to as miferable flaves as can
any where be found. But they contended for the prefent
actual equality of all men, with an exception to their own
flaves. And again, to fupport the argument, they were
obliged to fuppofe fociety diffolved, and men reduced to
that folitary, favage ftate, where fuch equality only can take
place. For fociety cannot be maintained, even in idea, but
by the inequality of condition, and the various ranks
neceffarily arifing from the focial compact.—So eafy is it for
men to take fuch parts of reafoning as beft fuit their prefent
purpofe.

temporary monopoly, the establishment of a certain staple or manufacture; nay, for purposes which respect the state, it may in certain points, and for a certain period, subject the person of one man to another, as in forming an army. But we cannot suppose a law that shall subject the person of one man to the private purposes of another, without once stipulating the extent of the authority, the nature of the service, or the sufficiency of the recompence. Such a law, by putting, perhaps, the greater part of the community out of the protection of all law, would be inconsistent with the notion of society. For the prime design of society is the extension of the operation of law and the equal treatment and protection of the citizens. Slavery, therefore, being the negation of law, cannot arise from law, or be compatible with it. As far as slavery prevails in any community, so far must that community be defective in answering the purposes of society. And this we affirm to be in the highest degree the case of our colonies. Slavery, indeed, in the manner wherein it is found there, is an unnatural state of oppression on the one side, and of suffering on the other; and needs only to be laid open or exposed in its native colours, to command the abhorrence and opposition of every man of feeling and sentiment.

SECT.

S E C T. II.

Mafter and Slave in ancient times.

WE are taught, by the higheft authority, that Mofes adapted feveral of his inftitutions to the particular difpofition of his countrymen. He did not attempt to prohibit flavery among them, perhaps, becaufe they were not then more ripe for it, than for the indiffoluble band of matrimony; but while he allowed them to make flaves of the conquered Canaanites and their pofterity, he endeavoured to render their lot eafy, and the behaviour of mafters humane. Indeed, in the early ages, it is a manner peculiar to him, and the Athenian legiflators, (of whom hereafter) to have paid in the cafe of flaves a proper attention to the referved and unalienable rights of human nature.

He enacts, that there fhould be one law, one rule of juftice for the native and for the ftranger; which is in direct oppofition to fome of our colony laws, where the evidence of even a free African will not be taken againft a white man. He fecures good ufage to the flave, by commanding, that if his mafter, in beating him, ftrike out but a fingle tooth, he fhall have his freedom. He ordains the perfonal flavery of every Jew to terminate in the beginning of the feventh, or fabbatical year, whether

near

near at hand, or diftant, when that commenced.
He guards effectually againft a groveling flavifh
fpirit among his people, by condemning him to
perpetual flavery, who, inticed by kind treatment from his mafter, fhould fhow a difregard
of this noble privilege of the fabbatical year.
He calls repeatedly on his people to remember,
that they themfelves had been flaves in Egypt ;
and, therefore, from motives of fellow-feeling
fhould make the condition of their flaves eafy
and agreeable to them. He bids them treat
well ftrangers of one country, becaufe they had
been ftrangers in their land; others, becaufe
they were of the fame lineage with themfelves.
He tells them, that the inftitution of a weekly
fabbath had in contemplation, the benevolent
purpofe of giving reft to the wearied flave, and
a refpite from toil, even to the wearied ox.

Among thofe nations that had not the light of
revelation to direct their conduct, the Athenians
deferve the firft place: they were indulgent,
eafy, and kind to their flaves, when compared
with their neighbours. And well this condefcenfion became a people, who, by mere force
of genius, advanced human nature much nearer
to perfection than any other nation. That their
good fenfe did not, in every particular, carry
them to that equality of behaviour towards their
flaves, which humanity might expect, or benevolence fuggeft, is not fo much to be wondered

at,

at, as that they fhould be able to oppofe the example of all their neighbours for capricious feverity, and in the chief lines of their conduct refpecting fuch ill-fated beings, fhould give occafion to the obfervation, that the life of a flave at Athens was much happier than that of a freeman in any other Grecian ftate.

If Athenian flaves were treated with cruelty by their mafters, they might claim protection in the Temple of Thefeus : there they remained in fafety till the fubject of complaint could be tried at law. Nor, in that cafe, did the law ruin, or refufe to relieve, thofe whom it pretended to affift ; for juftice was diftributed to rich and poor at the expence of the public. If the complaint of the flave was found to be juft, the mafter was obliged to affign over his fervice to fome other perfon. Slaves could demand an exchange of mafters, if their mafter had made any attempt on their chaftity. The law alfo gave them protection and remedy, in their own names and perfons, againft every injury that might have been done them by any citizen, not their mafter.

Athenian flaves were not reftrained in any of the common amufements of fociety. They were allowed to acquire property, on paying their mafters a certain yearly rate. If able to purchafe their freedom, they might demand it
of

of their mafter for a determined price. Their
mafters fometimes, the ftate often, rewarded
their fervice-and fidelity with freedom; in particular, after having been once employed in
war, they were fure to be made free. Contrary to the policy of modern times, the Athenians deemed no man fit to defend the ftate, but
him who was worthy to be a member of it.

The Athenians reaped the advantage of their
moderation and humanity. For though, by the
loweft calculation, their country contained
three grown male flaves for one freeman, notice
is taken, in their hiftory,.of only one infur-
rection among their miners; and once, in time
of war, of a confiderable number who deferted
from their mafters, and abandoned the country.
On the other hand, their neighbours, the Spar-
tans, who, through a wantonly cruel policy,
were continually haraffing, ill treating, oppreffing, nay, to keep their hands accuftomed
to blood, butchering their flaves, were held in
conftant alarms by them, and often were brought
into extreme danger, by their defperate attempts to regain their liberty. Yet the condition of flaves among the Spartans, from the
circumftance of their being generally the property of the public, and attached to the foil,
more readily admitted of univerfal relaxation
and indulgence, than it did among the Athenians,
where they were chiefly private property.

There

There is fuch a conformity, not only in thefe, but other particulars, between the laws of Mofes, enacted during the fabulous ages of Greece, and thefe laws, eftablifhed in its improved ftate, long after that time, by a people defervedly celebrated, as the beft cultivated, the moft fenfible, and humane among the ancient nations, as might have fecured to that great man a little more refpect than he in common meets with, among the wits and reafoners of the prefent age; who, while they deny his divine miffion, in that denial, muft acknowledge his forefight, his benevolence, his knowledge of the human heart, above every character in antiquity. For his laws continue, at this day, to be obeyed by a confiderable people, in the moft inconvenient circumftances, while all other laws of former ages are loft in the gulph of time, or are only to be found in fragments in old neglected books. *

In the infant ftate of Rome, flaves worked, and lived with their mafters, without much diftinction

---

* Even the law that abfolves a mafter for flaying his flave, in the cafe of his not dying till two days after the ftroke, bears a ftrong analogy to that tendernefs in the common law of England, that diftinguifhes between homicide and murder, and, as it were loth to find the culprit guilty, takes the deadlinefs of the weapon into account; and it fhews, that among the Jews, the magiftrate interpofed between the mafter and his flave; which, in fome of our colonies, has not been the cafe, even when fhocking circumftances of murder have loudly called for it.

diſtinction of rank or uſage. But in proportion as luxury increaſed among the Romans, the condition of their ſlaves ſunk gradually down to the loweſt degree of wretchedneſs and miſery. And indeed ſuch repreſentations as the ſtatue of the dying gladiator, which exhibits the life of a brave uſeful man ſacrificed, not to the ſafety of his country, but to the barbarous whim of, perhaps, the moſt worthleſs ſet of men that ever were aſſembled together in one place;* the ſcandalous traffic that the elder Cato carried on in the natural feelings of his ſlaves, his ſetting them adrift to ſtarve in their old age,† when

* In what an amiable point of view doth the following incident place the Athenians, even in their latter degenerate ſtate? Some ſycophants of the Romans, then their maſters, had propoſed to them, in a public aſſembly, to imitate their lords, in the exhibition of ſhows of prize fighters, and gladi- ators in their theatres. A worthy citizen, who was preſent, affected to applaud the flattering meaſure, and requeſted his fellow-citizens only firſt to accompany him and help him to throw down the altar, which, in their better times, they had erected to mercy. That ſenſible people felt immediately the grave rebuke; and were the only ſtate in Greece, that had courage to forbear imitating the barbarity of their conquerors.

† How inconſiſtent with himſelf is man. He, who, in his own conduct, could debaſe himſelf by ſuch acts of meanneſs and cruelty, when Cenſor, degraded Lucius, the brother of Flaminius, becauſe he had indulged the capricious curioſity of a favourite boy, with the ſcene of a man dying a violent death, in the perſon of a ſlave, whom, for that purpoſe, he ſlew with his own hand.—The traffic referred to above, was his locking up his female ſlaves, and hiring them out, by the night, to ſuch males as could lay down a certain price for them.

when they could no longer be ferviceable to him, the condemning of them to fifh-ponds for trivial faults ; all thefe things muft fill every reflecting man with fuch abhorrence of, and indignation at, the conduct of the Romans, in the character of mafters, in their advanced ftate of empire, as muft prove them unworthy of being drawn into example, except to be execrated for their conduct. While they fancied themfelves lords of the world, they forgot that they were men ; while they indulged their amufement, they ftifled their humanity. Indeed, what could be expected from a people capable of receiving a law, that, according to the ufual interpretation of it, in a cafe of infolvency, ordained a fellow-citizen to be cut piece-meal, and be divided among his creditors ?

But how miferable the condition of flaves in general was among the ancients, may be collected from the opinion and example of that benevolent and difcreet philofopher, Plutarch, who yet has very freely cenfured the inhuman behaviour of others. He affures us, that the only effectual way of managing a flave is by the difcipline of the whip ; that a flave is incapable of underftanding any arguments, except ftripes, and a chain. And agreeably to this opinion he is introduced to us, as in a characteriftic action of his life, fhewing how coolly a philofopher could flea the back of a poor

friendlefs,

friendlefs, helplefs wretch. * ˉFarther, De-
mofthenes, who, in every thing refpecting the
freedom, and character of his country, feems
infpired with the very genius of liberty, lays it
down as a maxim not to be controverted, that
the higheft evidence, and teftimony moft to be
depended on, is what is forced out of a flave
by torture.

Adrian is the firft on record, who, by an
edict, deprived the mafter of the power of life
and death in his family. As the benevolence of
the Chriftian religion, about his time, had fecretly, ˈyet univerfally, infinuated itfelf into
the fentiments, and tinctured the reafoning, of
the learned; and as he was more fond of the
                                        title

---

* The hiftory is this: He had ordered the flave to be corrected. The fellow muttered; and obferved, that a man,
like his mafter, who pretended to act the Philofopher, and to
hold all his paffions and affections equally poifed, behaved in
a manner unbecoming his character, when, on any poffible
provocation, he fell into fuch a paffion with a poor flave, as
could be fatiated only by flafhing and cutting him unmercifully
with a whip. Plutarch, quibbling with the wretch, obferves,
in anfwer, that paffion generally had marks by which its prefence was denoted: an elevated tone, a flufhing countenance,
a threatening look; could he have any of thefe, or the violence that they expreffed, who argued the matter with all the
calmnefs of a ftoic. ˈAnd as the executioner had interrupted
his ftrokes, waiting for the iffue of the difcourfe, he coolly
bids him proceed in his method of inculcating knowledge by
the whip, while he and Syrus difcuffed the fubject philofo-
phically. But a man muft have fpent fome time in the
fouthern provinces of North America, or our fugar colonies,.
to be able to imagine the fcene.

title of Philofopher than of Emperor, it is beyond conjecture, that this edict, at that particular time, owed its origin to revealed religion; and within a fhort period after this, perfonal flavery, by the fame influence, was abolifhed throughout the empire. *

S E C T. III.

Mafter and Slave in Gothic Times.

THE inundation of the northern nations, that broke into the Roman Empire, and the feudal tenures that were introduced by it, gave rife to a new fpecies of flavery in Europe, the remains of which are yet to be found, particularly

---

* Raynall afferts, that the abolition of flavery and Paganifm, by edict, in the time of Conftantine, brought on the ruin of the Roman Empire. Doubtlefs every violent change in a ftate, muft bring danger with it. But, perhaps, it will be difficult for any, but a modern philofopher, who follows Hume in his paradoxes, to conceive how the extenfion of fentiment and freedom fhould fpread ruin among a people. That empire had begun to nod to its fall, long before this change could have produced any effect. The univerfal degeneracy of manners, the contempt of religion, the prevalence of Epicurean notions, the difregard of national character, the effeminacy of the foldiers, their lofs of difcipline, the inftability of the government, and the natural courfe of human grandeur, are fufficient to account for the downfal of that fabric, under the rude fhock of furrounding favages. That Chriftianity produced this effect of abolifhing flavery, is the opinion alfo of Fletcher; for which fee Sect. IV. of this chapter.

C

cularly in Denmark and Poland. But it appears, that, in general, this flavery confifted in obliging the conquered nations to cultivate their own lands, and render to the conquerors fuch a part of the produce as they thought proper to afcertain. This condition naturally connected the labourers with the foil which they cultivated; and it rofe into a cuftom to transfer them together from one proprietor to another: and, doubtlefs, there were many reduced alfo to the condition of domeftic flaves. But, like the Swedifh prifoners made at the battle of Pultowa, they became the teachers and reformers of their mafters. And as thefe were by degrees converted to religion and won to civilized life, fo this ftate of fubordination went on approaching gradually to the condition of equality, or rather of that reciprocal focial dependence, which we have fhewn muft exift between the fervant and mafter. And among the many fad things that we every day hear of popes, priefts, and prieftcraft, this muft be acknowledged to their credit, (they are indeed charged with it by their enemies) that their influence was conftantly ufed with the converts, to procure the manumiffion, or at leaft the humane treatment of their flaves. Such has been conftantly the natural effect of Chriftianity, in every poffible form, to favour perfonal as well as mental liberty, till the gradual improvement of fociety, the extenfion of fentiment, and fluctuation of property, become

come fufficient to change perfonal flavery into a voluntary compact of fervice and fidelity on the one fide, of wages and protection on the other : a compact, which fuppofeth that ftate of mutual dependence effential to polifhed fo-ciety, and which may be confidered as entering originally into the plan thereof, and I truft is not intirely out of fight in the cafe of which we treat. *

Indeed this latter flavery, in its worft ftate, muft, after the converfion of the mafters, have been far preferable to the ancient flavery of the heathens, or the modern flavery of the negroes in the European colonies. The Chriftian flaves of Chriftian mafters were confidered as entitled to certain rights, on which a mafter could not encroach : particularly, the making of the ce-remony of marriage a religious folemnity, and its obligations of confequence indiffoluble, ex-cept by death, drew after it all the claims and rights of a family. Their worfhipping at the fame altar, and their being confidered as entitled, equally with their mafters, to all the fpiritual advantages annexed to the profeffion of Chrifti-anity, were circumftances which the priefts were careful to ufe to the beft advantage in

their

* The Banians in India are at this day, fupplied with flaves from Abyffinia. But as foon as they are brought home, they are treated as children of the family ; they are inftructed in fome ufeful trade ; they are allowed to raife families, and maintain them with the profits of their labour, with which the mafter meddles not.

their favour : and, in an age, wherein the promifes and threats of religion influenced, at
leaft, the outward conduct of the people, and
its doctrines made generally a part of the reafoning in ufe ; * when its minifters were held in
honour, and their injunctions carried with them
reverence and authority for their Mafter's fake,
thefe were effectual and prevailing topics. The
people alfo reaped advantages from thefe difputes between the kings and their barons.
Kings favoured the liberty of burghers and
peafants, becaufe every individual abfolved of his
allegiance to a baron, was an auxiliary detached
from an enemy or rival lord. †

Had Europe, as a much diftinguifhed quarter of the globe, reaped no other focial advantage
from the eftablifhment of Chriftianity than the
abolition

.* This is exceedingly well exemplified in what is called the
truce of God or the church, when the fabbaths, and folemn
times, and feftivals of the church, gave a refpite to thofe cruel
depredations and murders that each village-tyrant or lord of a
caftle, thofe former felf-erected legiflators, thought himfelf
permitted, at other times, to perpetrate among his neighbours.

† Though, in many cafes, this was only changing one tyrant for another ; yet the people favoured the meafure, becaufe
they have conftantly found an oppreffor intolerable in the inverfe ratio of his rank and extent of power. " A poor man,
" oppreffing the poor," faith Solomon, " is like a fweeping
" rain," he leaves no food. To give fecurity to the members
of any ftate, the community muft be of that extent and power
which will make it refpectable among its neighbours ; and its
governors muft be removed fo far from the level of other citizens, that private intereft or refentment may not fenfibly influence their public conduct. · But this can hardly ever be
the cafe in fmall ftates.

abolition of flavery, this benefit alone would have been immenfe; the fuperiority gained by it over the reft of the world would have been incredible. And with what fhame and forrow muft we remark, that fhe, who has been raifed fo high above her fellows, by the influence of this heaven-defcended liberty, at this day is, and, for more than two centuries paft, has been, ftriving with all the venturous energy of a commercial fpirit, to eftablifh flavery in the new world; in a region, where the curfe of flavery was unknown, till, through an infernal love of gold, fhe introduced and fixed it? But when the Englifh, (for though the Portuguefe and Spaniards had tranfported Africans more early to their American fettlements; yet Hawkins, an Englifhman, is faid firft to have given occafion for the prefent inhuman trade) a nation moft highly favoured of liberty, is viewed as taking the lead in this odious traffic, and as berding down the foul in utter darknefs, the more effectually to enflave the body; freedom muft blufh indignantly, while humanity mourns over the reproachful tale. * Would God we might indulge

* It muft fill the reader with very ferious reflections, to be told, that, fince the year 1759, the Britifh African trade has been, in a great proportion, turned to the fupplying of the French iflands with flaves. This has given a moft rapid improvement to their fugar plantations; and there is laid a foundation for fuch a naval force, as if not guarded againft in time may avenge humanity on our nation for this fhocking traffic, which it has carried on to a greater extent than all the reft of Europe, with peculiar circumftances of barbarity and cruelty.

indulge the hope, that the fame people, who firſt riveted, might alfo firſt cut aſunder, the iron chain which difgraces our nature and nation, in the weſtern world ; and that a people, who have rifqued their own exiſtence, frequently, as a ſtate, to keep one continental tyrant from ridding the world of another, might at laſt have wifdom to render themſelves rich and powerful, by reſtoring to liberty, and recovering to ſociety and reaſon, the exiled ſons of Africa. *

But

* In the month of March 1783, the following circumſtances came out in the trial of a caſe of inſurance at Guildhall. An ignorant maſter of a ſlave-ſhip had overſhot his port, Jamaica, and was afraid of wanting water before he could beat up again to the iſland. He himſelf fell ſick. In the courſe of his illneſs, he ordered his mate, who was the man that gave the evidence, to throw overboard 46 ſlaves, hand-cuffed ; and he was readily obeyed. Two days after he ordered 36 more to be thrown after them, and after two days more another parcel of 40. Ten others, who had been permitted to take the air on deck, unfettered, jumped into the ſea indignantly after them. The ſhip, after all, brought into port 480 gallons of water. Can humanity imagine that it was meant, in any poſſible circumſtances, to ſubmit the fate of ſuch numbers of reaſonable creatures to the reveries of a ſick monſter ; or that his brutal inſtrument ſhould dare to boaſt of his obedience, and even do it with impunity, in the higheſt criminal court of the beſt informed people of Europe ?

The Incas of Peru conquered to poliſh and improve. When they came to a brutiſh people, who could not readily apprehend their inſtructions, Let us turn, ſaid they, from theſe incorrigible animals, and ſeek out a people worthy of being our ſcholars. The ſavages of America are ſo wholly without the conception of the poſſibility of one man's being ſubmitted to the

But before I confider flavery as it has been introduced and eftablifhed by Europeans in the weftern world, I fhall lay before the reader a plan of that celebrated friend to liberty, Fletcher, of Saltoun, for reducing his country back into the ancient ftate of mafter and flave, in order to obviate fome temporary inconveniences imagined to arife from freedom. And as he does this with an appearance of reafoning, and, indeed, fuggefts things that would be exceedingly proper to be attended to, in the firft dawnings of

the will of another, that they know no medium between roafting their prifoners, and adopting them into their families. The Europeans, fettled in the fame country, could traverfe the vaft Atlantic to traffis for, enflave, and fell, wretches unknown to them, who never injured them; nay, could keep working in iron chains their own unhappy countrymen fent among them : while they boaft of having vindicated for themfelves, as the natural inheritance of freedom, a total independence on all authority not originating from themfelves. Reafon, as found in practice among men, is but a name, when feparated from intereft.—It is but juftice due to the Weft Indian proprietors to obferve, that the planters of tobacco and rice, in America, in common, not only treated their African flaves and Englifh convicts, but even fober, honeft people, who, to pay for their paffage from Europe, had been obliged to fell their fervice for five years, with full as much feverity as was practifed only on Africans in the fugar iflands ; and, what was inexcufable, in a country where provifions coft labour only, even pinched them in their food. Indented fervants were tied up, and lafhed cruelly on the moft trifling occafions. They were made to drag iron rings of ten or twelve pounds weight, hammered round their ancles, and fleep as they could with heavy iron chains and crooks round their necks.

of liberty; I shall at once confider his propofal, and add fuch obfervations as naturally arife from it.

S E C T.   IV.

Mafter and Slave, as propofed for Scotland,
Anno 1698.

SOON after the revolution, Scotland was af-flicted with four or five fucceffive unfruitful years, that, in its then improvident method of agriculture, reduced it to a ftate of famine, which is ftill remembered under the name of the *Dear Years.* Many died of want, and thoufands, all over the country, were reduced to beggary; the Highlanders, efpecially, fuffered greatly, and came down and overfpread the low-lands; and, where they did not fucceed by begging, made no fcruple to fteal and rob, to fupply their wants. In this fituation of things, when the poor were numerous, few manu-factures eftablifhed, and the fifheries lay ne-glected, did Fletcher propofe his plan of flavery, founding it on a ftatute enacted Anno 1579, which empowered any fubject of fufficient eftate to take the child of any beggar, and educate him for his own fervice, for a certain term of years, which term was extended Anno 1597 for life.

He

He obferves, that hiftory makes no mention of poor or beggars in ancient times, becaufe all the poor, being flaves, were maintained by their own mafters. He fays, no modern ftate, except Holland, by the aid of its manufactures, has been able to employ or maintain its poor: that this new burthen has been brought on fociety by churchmen, who either by miftake or defign have confounded things fpiritual and temporal, and all good order, and good government, by recommending it to mafters to fave their fouls, by fetting at liberty fuch of their flaves as fhould embrace the Chriftian faith; in contradiction to our Saviour, who was far from ufing temporal advantages to enforce eternal truths; and to St. Paul, who, 1 Cor. vii. pofitively gives the preference to flavery. Hence we date hofpitals, alms-houfes, and contributions; burdens, which we find fo heavy on the community, and fo inadequate to the purpofe.

He ftates the common objections urged againft flavery; that men are equal by nature; that it is unjuft to fubmit the feelings and happinefs of the major part of a community, to the oppreffion and barbarity of the few; and that the tyrant, who enflaves his country, has the fame plea for profecuting his ambitious views, that a rich man can offer for bringing his fellows into bonbage to him.

C 5

He

He anfwers thefe by diftinguifhing between
political and domeftic flavery, affirming that the
latter has been difgraced, by having been confounded with the other, which alone deferves
the name of flavery, as being fubmitted, not to
law, which may regulate domeftic flavery, but
to a jealous tyrant's caprice: that it is the
intereft of every mafter to ufe his flaves well,
in order that he may reap the full advantage of
their labour: that occafional deviations from
the fuggeftions of this prudence may be prevented by proper laws and regulations, and by
the watchful care of a judge appointed for that
purpofe.

He fhews the advantages which would accompany this eftablifhment, by ftating what was
the cafe in ancient times. The ancients had no
poor caft loofe on the public. They could,
without poffeffing much other wealth, under-
take, with their flaves, great public and private
works: and this manner of employing their
flaves and their wealth, preferved among them
a fimplicity of manners, and living, not otherwife to be accounted for. Mafters knew
nothing of the vexation of hired fervants, who,
after having been educated at a great expence
for a man's fervice, will leave him on the moft
trifling occafion. Their flaves, in hopes of
obtaining their liberty, had an emulation to
pleafe; and their being able to poffefs nothing,
took

took away that temptation to pilfer, fo commonly the propenfity of hired fervants, and, indeed, fometimes rendered neceffary for them to fupport their families.

He propofeth that vagabonds, and fuch poor as cannot maintain themfelves, be proportioned out to men of a certain eftate, to be employed in their grounds, that their children be brought up to fuch ufeful manufactures as can be carried on at home ; and that the public may not, in any cafe, lofe the benefit of their labour, they and their children fhall be transferable for ever. *

He

---

* Vagabond beggars are a nuifance which call loudly for redrefs, and which every well regulated fociety will exert itfelf to get rid of. Let every vagabond be confidered as the property of the public. Let a day be fixed, by proclamation, for apprehending them throughout the kingdom. Let their fervice be fold for feven years to fuch as have employment for them. Let the money got for the ftrong be given with the weak. If, at the expiration of their flavery, they fhew a difpofition to fettle, and can make a private bargain with any reponfible perfon, who will anfwer to the public for their behaviour, and will take them to work on the footing of free labourers, let them be difcharged. This will excite them to be honeft and faithful. Slavery, except for a crime that forfeits life, fhould not be for life, that it may not perpetuate flavery in their children. Every vagabond child fhould be brought up to fome ufeful calling, and be free at thirty years of age. They all, when reftored to freedom, fhould be allowed a fettlement.

A particular magiftrate fhould fuperintend their treatment, hear, and decide on their and their mafters complaints. If at the termination of any period of flavery, they be found unworthy

He thinks the master should not have power over the life of his servant, but should answer for it with his own. He should not torture or mutilate him : if convicted of such ill treatment, he should free his slave, and fix a pension on him.

worthy of freedom, let them be sold anew. If purchasers do not offer, let them be divided by lot, and their children be apprentices. Coarse, wholesome food should be allotted them, the kind and minimum being fixed by law.

If parishes were obliged to improve their commons, there would be full employment for them; and every thief, being first marked, should be added to the number. When restored to freedom, they might have a cottage and garden given them, in full right, which they may prepare during the time of their servitude.

Such a state would be far beyond the condition of a vagabond, a wretch, that regards neither divine nor human laws, but wallows in every impurity and low vice. These regulations, properly pursued for one generation, would annihilate the evil; the very dread of being sold, and working at the will of another, would recover the greatest part of them to labour and society. But this remedy should be strictly confined to thieves and vagabonds, and only while they continued such.

At present our poor laws are calculated to encourage laziness, by supporting an idle man in as much plenty as him who labours and gets his bread honestly. When sick, the poor should be tenderly cared for; but when only idle they should have a scanty coarse fare, and clothes made up of patches, to make their situation irksome to them. Those that have large families should have every reasonable indulgence, and the burden of their children should be made easy to them. All single strollers should be strictly dealt with. Wherever the indolence of those that are supported by charity is suspected, their pittance should not be given in money, but in food, from day to day; and there should, as in hospitals, be rates of full, half, and third allowance.

him. The fervant's family fhould be provided for in clothes, diet, and lodging. His children fhould be inftructed in the principles of morality and religion, be taught to read, and be furnifhed with proper books. They fhall not work on Sundays ; but have liberty to go to church. In every circumftance, but that of not poffeffing property, and their labour being directed at the will of another, they fhall not be under the rule of their mafters, but the protection of the law. When grown, by age, ufelefs to their mafters, they fhall be received into public hofpitals. If their mafter, on any account, make them free, he fhall either accommodate them with a penfion, or put them in a way of living, that will keep them from becoming burdenfome to the public. To check the abufe of power in the mafter, a magiftrate fhould be appointed to fee that juftice be done them.

Now, however inadmiffible fuch a ftate of fervitude may be, in a country where liberty is the eftablifhed birth-right of the loweft member of the community, yet, would heaven, that the flavery in our fugar colonies were only what is here propofed. We muft then drop many of our objections againft it. Still the arguments againft this degree of it are unanfwerable.

He fuppofeth that a fenfe of intereft will prevent the abufe of power in the mafter. There cannot

cannot be a fairer deduction in theory, (which was all that he could have to go upon) nor is there one more falfe in fact. Even fhould we afcribe the treatment which Africans meet with from their mafters, not wholly to an abufe of power, but, in fome meafure, alfo to a perfuafion, whether it be true or falfe, that becaufe of their inferiority we are not obliged to treat them well ; how comes it that fober, indented, white fervants, are treated with equal, perhaps fuperior cruelty by their North American mafters ; in confequence of which, not more than one in five furvives even a temporary flavery of five years, in a condition to fettle a habitation and family for himfelf ? Revenge for contradiction or faults in an inferior, whether real or imagined, will not allow the cooler affections of the mind to operate, but drives at once, like an eagle on its helplefs prey, heedlefs how far the avenger himfelf may be involved in the mifchief.

Nor, though his magiftrate be an exceeding proper and neceffary check, would he, or could he, if ever fo impartial and watchful, be able to enfure good ufage to fervants, from the ignorant, the parfimonious, the luxurious, the extravagant, the capricious, the paffionate, the fpiteful mafter. In a thoufand ways may they be, and they daily are, tormented, which no law can provide againft, no care can poffibly remedy.

His

His diftinction between political and domeftic flavery, except wherein they refpect different objects, is imaginary and inconclufive, when applied to individuals ; or whatever difference there is, will be found to conclude againft the latter. The great tyrant has not the opportunity of exercifing his luft of oppreffion over individuals, except they ftand oppofed to his power ; and a quiet man may, in an extenfive country, pafs his time tolerably eafy and fecure under the moft arbitrary government. But the domeftic tyrant can teafe and torment every wretch fubmitted to his power, every moment of their lives. They cannot eat or fleep, but when and how he pleafeth. Every feeling, every indulgence, is held at his pleafure ; and too often he feels a fpiteful amufement, an infernal delight, in unneceffarily imbittering their miferable cup, even at the expence of his own eafe and intereft.

That the heavenly Preacher of peace and good will towards men, fhould be fuppofed to have encouraged an unnatural ftate of fociety, which, in its very inftitution, muft counteract in the fuperior every benevolent inclination from man to man; and muft go far to fupprefs in the inferior every defire after that intellectual improvement, and heavenly happinefs, to point out the way to which was the very defign of his humiliation ; is fuch blafphemy againft the divine

goodnefs

goodnefs and condefcenfion of his miſſion, and is ſo flatly contradicted by the whole tenor of his doctrine, as to be utterly unworthy of any anfwer. St. Paul again is preſſed into the ſervice of ſlavery, againſt the plain grammatical ſenfe of the expreſſion in the original, and the whole fcope of his argument : of ſo much more weight than truth is the driving of a favourite point. After generally remarking, that, notwithſtanding any ſuppofed particular inconveniences, political happinefs, by the extenſion of freedom, has been extended far beyond what the warmeſt imagination could conceive; we may allow churchmen in the company of their Maſter and his apoſtle, to reſt ſatisfied with the blame of having been the means of aboliſhing ſlavery; and may hope that this writer's authority, in this cafe, may ſtand them in ſome ſtead againſt that more general reproach caſt on them of their being the worſhippers of power in whatever hands it is found.

By depriving a fervant of property, as he propofes, we know, that, in fact, you make him carelefs and defperate. The beſt way of fecuring his fidelity and honeſty, is to contrive that he may have property to care for and fear the lofs of. If a ſlave has deferted the plantation, the moſt effectual way to bring him back is to give out, that you mean, if he does not return, by ſuch a day, to pull his houfe down.

He

He remarks that the Highlanders of his days were savage thieves and beggars, becaufe fubject to their chieftans; and would not his eftablifhment of the like fubjection in the civilized low-lands, in time produce the like effects? A Chriftian would refolve the filence concerning the poor in the heathen world, to their not being deemed an object either of hiftory or philofophy; or to that common tie between man and man, which revelation inculcates, not being then acknowledged, to make the relief of their diftrefs a matter of duty or merit.

But if no poor were then fupported by private benevolence, was no mifery therefore felt? What were the early feditions at Rome, but ftruggles between wealth and poverty, till war and diftant conqueft had enriched or drawn off the oppreffed ftarving multitude? Indeed, where was there room left for public beggars, when the poor were flaves, and had only their mafters to whom to cry for help? Yet the elder Cato turned out fome beggars on the public, in a manner not greatly to his credit. Among the Jews, the rigours of flavery were foftened by religion; and there the poor, from the firft, were an object of law. Their law-givers informed them, that in their moft flourifhing ftate, there fhould be always poor among them, whom they were to confider as the Lord's penfioners, who were in his name to receive,
from

from their wealthy neighbours, that tribute of grateful thanks which his goodnefs claimed from them. And, doubtlefs, had this duty been pro-pofed, from the like motives, in other ftates, proper objects of it would not have been found wanting.

A better reafon to be given for the fimpli-city of the ancient manner of living may be found in the little communication which there was between different countries for the purpofe of exchanging modes and fuperfluities. Thofe who live now on the produce of their own grounds, live as uniformly, and fimply as the ancients did. But was the Roman mode fimple after the conqueft of Afia? He mentions the public works of the ancients. Do we know thofe of any ftate that in grandeur or utility may be compared to the floating fortreffes of Britain, which carry the arms and power of the ftate around the world?

Why the public fhould build hofpitals to receive flaves, worn down in the fervice of private perfons, he gives not a reafon; nor is any obvious. If the ancients were not troubled with the reftlefs ingratitude and pilfering habits of hired fervants, did they feel no inconveniency from the fullen intractable difpofition of flaves, whom they could not get rid of? Or, if the defire of freedom excited the emulation of a
flave,

flave, would it not make him alfo feel the immediate hardfhips of flavery? would he not, with defpair, look around him, and view many flaves transferred from one mafter to another; often from good to bad, without acquiring that liberty which they had endeavoured to deferve by their fidelity? and would he not anticipate the like fate, and lofe all defire of exertion? Is not this indeed the general cafe, at this day, in the fugar colonies?

Fletcher fuppofes that neceffity will drive his country into the meafure of flavery. It is near a century fince he hazarded this opinion; and inftead thereof, by the abolifhing of jurifdictions, more liberty, and greater privileges have been communicated to it: and the confequence has been a more general extenfion of political happinefs, and private conveniency. Had his plan taken place, would fo many towns have arifen, or been enlarged in various parts of the country? Should we have heard of the manufactures at Paifly? Could Glafgow have been able to have endured a lofs (even fuppofing it only temporary) of perhaps a million of money, by American independency, almoft without once complaining? Would a few overgrown landlords have allowed the Britifh army and navy to have been filled up and recruited out of their gangs of flaves, by the many ten thoufands of Scotchmen, that in every war, fince his time, have

bled

bled fometimes for the rights of the empire, fometimes to quiet the popular alarms, about that bugbear, the balance of power? Would oppreffed, half ftarved flaves have made fuch hardy foldiers; or, like them, endured, without complaint, every various oppofite climate, in carrying on the public fervice?

It is true Scotland ftill labours under difadvantages. The tenant is not fufficiently fecured againft the extortion of the landlord. But what would be gained by reducing a great porportion of thefe tenants and their pofterity into the condition of flaves? Would they be allowed to live plentifully, when their lords wanted to parade it at court? Or are luxury and extravagance to be fatisfied, while any thing within their reach remains to be devoured? If flavery had been eftablifhed on his plan, would not power and intrigue have been ufed, to draw within its circle as many as poffible, till mafter and flave had abforbed every other rank? No, let lazinefs and vice be effectually reftrained, even by reftraining that liberty and privileges which they juftly forfeit. But fet not one man paramount over another. Let their country and its laws remain mafters of their fate.

S E C T.

S E C T. V.

Maſter and Slave in the French Colonies.

I N the French colonies, the public pays an immediate attention to the treatment and inſtruction of ſlaves. The intendants are charged with their protection, proper miſſionaries are appointed for the purpoſe of training them up to a certain degree of religious knowledge; and ample eſtates or funds are allotted for the maintenance of thoſe eccleſiaſtics. The negroes, as ſoon as introduced into the colony, are put under the care of theſe laſt. The maſter is obliged to acquaint the governor or intendant, within eight days, of every African ſlave whom he has purchaſed, that a miſſionary may be aſſigned to inſtruct him. All the faſts and feſtivals of the Romiſh church, which it is well known are very numerous, are commanded to be ſtrictly obſerved, during which the ſlave is forbidden to labour, that he may have leiſure to attend maſs.

Every ſlave has a claim to a certain allowance of food and clothing, which is not to be diminiſhed by their maſters, under pretence of having given him time to work for himſelf. The power of the maſter is reſtrained to the whip and chain; he may not wound or mutilate his ſlave. On ill treatment received from his
maſter,

master, or on being deprived of his allowance
of food and raiment, the slave is directed to apply to the King's attorney, who is obliged to
prosecute the master forthwith. This officer is
also bound to prosecute, if by any other means
he hears of the abuse. This reason is added in
the law, " This we will to be observed, to
" check the abuse of power in the master." If
a slave rendered unserviceable, through age,
hurts, or disease, be turned adrift by his master,
he is to be placed in the public hospital, and to
be maintained there at the expence of his
master. These are some of the regulations established by the Code Noir, to check the exor-
bitancy of masters ; an instance of attention and
benevolence in the French government, that
may well put British negligence to shame !

The respect in which marriage is held, brings
a farther advantage to French slaves. The ceremony is solemnized by the priest, and the tie
continues for life. This gives them an attachment to their little families, and a concern for
their interest, and of consequence a care over
them, and their own behaviour, that is seldom
seen among English slaves ; where the connexion
between the sexes is arbitrary, and too frequently casual ; where a male slave reckons it a
piece of state to multiply his wives, and
change them at pleasure, without looking beyond
the present gratification, or considering how his
conduct

conduct may affect the fate of his offspring. Care is alfo taken in the French iflands to marry them young, in the fame plantation; and if they perceive a particular attachment between two young people, belonging to different mafters, it is common to refign or exchange them, that they may both have the fame owner, and that marriage may have its full effect on their conduct. *

The French flaves reap a confiderable advantage from the prefence of their owners. One caufe of this is, that, in the colonies, they enjoy more liberty, and pay fewer taxes than in France. † An Englifh planter, if out of debt,

or

* A gentleman of Guadaloupe, Monfieur Seguer, informed me, that, with fome pains, he had brought it about to have all his flaves married within his own plantations; and that by making them all people of _property, in allowing to each his bit of land, with a hog, a goat, and fome poultry, and by fome extraordinary pains ufed to inftruct them, he had brought them to a degree of healthinefs, good fenfe, tractability, and happinefs uncommon among his neighbours. And I fhall here remark, generally, that nothing has a happier effect in reforming or improving a flave, than the giving him fomething of his own to care for, and fear the lofs of.

† The French governors have liberal appointments from the crown to fet them above the neceffity, and to take away the temptation of oppreffing their people by exacting extraordinary fees from them in the manner of our Weft Indian governors, who, to the difgrace of the government that appointed them, are forced to collect their maintenance in perquifites from thofe who have bufinefs with them. The Britifh colonies

are

or a cafual crop be plentiful, muft run away to England, which he calls his home, where generally loft to every ufeful purpofe in life, he vies with the nobility in entertainments, extravagance, and expence, while his attorney, and manager, are obliged to over-work, and pinch, his poor flaves, to keep up, or increafe the ufual remittances. It would make indignation herfelf almoft fmile to hear their piteous complaining letters to their agents read, when the neceffities of the plantation have occafioned a fmall draught

to

are alfo made the property of patent officers, the profit of whofe places confifts wholly in perquifites, and is in general farmed from the principals in England by two or three fubftitutes in fucceffion, till the immediate poffeffor be obliged, in his own defence, to commit acts of oppreffion, to make up his rent. And fuch is the corrupt influence at our court of thefe finecure patentees, as to have procured a ftanding inftruction to governors to oppofe and render null every attempt made by provincial affemblies to regulate their fees of office, or check their extortion. Thus the government of the mother country is deprived of the affiftance of men of character and fubftance in public offices, to fupport its influence in the colonies; while thefe have impofed on them a moft humiliating and burdenfome badge of flavery, and have all their interefts, and all improvements of their police facrificed to the felfifh views of men whom they never faw. It has alfo been ufual of late years to permit the cuftom-houfe officers to hold their places by deputies, doubtlefs, to the great improvement of the revenue. The intercourfe between our Weft Indian colonies is by fmall veffels carrying £40 or £50 freight. The cuftom-houfes force full one half of this fum out of them, under the name of (not taxes but) fees. The confequence is, that when provifions or ftores are unloaded in one ifland, they cannot, but in extreme neceffity, be refhipped for another ifland.

to be made on them. And often the manager, whom the caprice, or felfifh, or family views of an attorney can, without warning, difplace, looks not forward to the confequences of ill treatment of flaves, while trying to recommend himfelf by a forced exertion of their ftrength, in hopes that its pernicious effects may poffibly not appear in his time.* If the Englifh owner lives on his plantation, he is too often fo involved in debt, the effects of his predeceffor's, or his own former extravagance, or of injudicious purchafes, that he can fpare little from the preffing demands of his creditors, to allot for the eafe, and well-being of flaves, or indeed for any neceffary improvement of his property. The French, as they generally live each on his own plantation, fo they are happy in not having the credit, or opportunity which the Englifh have of running in debt. † All their improvements

* Hence a planter always knows the ftate of his affairs beft, at the change of managers; it generally requiring many hundreds, fometimes thoufands of pounds, to fet matters agoing under the new director; an expence that might be faved by ufing a lefs parcimonious method in the ordinary management of the plantation.

† The whole debt owing by the Martinico planters about the year 1773 was eftimated nearly at 200,000l. fterling. St. Chriftopher's, which, in proportion to its extent, is our richeft colony, and may be in value about one-third of the importance of Martinico, though divided among fewer than 120 proprietors, could not owe lefs at that time than 720,000l. fterling.

D

ments muft arife out of their induftry. They
are therefore more gradual, and better founded,
than in our colonies, where it has been only neceffary to deliver in to a merchant an exag-
gerated, pompous account of the richnefs of the
plantation on which the money is to be raifed,
to procure liberty for drawing on him for thoufands after thoufands. Formerly induftry, in a
courfe of years, raifed immenfe fortunes in the
Weft Indies ; few have been raifed fince loans
became frequent in England. Borrowed money,
feldom, one may fay hardly ever, has fucceeded,
when in any confiderable proportion to the property mortgaged for it. Let others explain the
caufe, I content myfelf with recording the fact.
Thus French planters, not having intereft money
to provide, nor the ambition of retiring to Europe, to ftimulate them in accumulating money,
are not under the neceffity of forcing their flaves
beyond their ftrength, in carrying on their
plantations to that exquifite degree of culture,
that is common in our colonies, and which is
effected, not fo much by contrivance and method, or by increafing with proper care and
nourifhment the animal powers of their flaves,
as by obliging them to extraordinary efforts,
that foon wear them out ; and which, inftead
of allowing them to increafe in the courfe of
nature, make conftant demands on the flave
market, to enable them to fupport the character
of

of the plantation. Far from planting, as we do,
every rood of land that they poffefs, in fugar
cane, and depending on foreign fupplies for food,
the French try to live as much as poffible within
themfelves. A confiderable proportion of land
is fet apart for provifions. A late edict has re-
ftricted the minimum to one acre in ten. Farther, the French plantation flaves are attached
to the foil, and cannot be drawn off to pay
debts, or be fold feparate from it. This gives
them a lafting property in their huts, and little
fpots of ground. They may fafely cultivate
them, and not, as in the Britifh colonies, fear
their being turned out of poffeffion, or transferred from one proprietor to another, without
regard had to their intereft or feelings. From
thefe circumftances, and from their manners
being more communicative, the French, in the
colonies, live more in a family way among their
flaves, than our planters; they become more
fenfible of their wants and abilities; they naturally contract a regard and an affection for
them; the flaves are not hurried in their work,
and enjoy a greater plenty, and variety of whole-
fome food, than when their allowance of mufty
flour, or weavily maize from America, is dealt
out to them from a fcanty, bruifed tin or pew-
ter meafure, by an unfeeling overfeer; who
perhaps recommends himfelf to his abfent employer

ployer by the number of fhares into which he has divided the wretched pittance. *

Now the obfervation is, that the French flaves are more decently dreffed, are more orderly, fenfible, and ten times more honeft than Englifh flaves. They ufe private prayer. The field negroes begin and leave off work with prayer; the black overfeer officiating as prieft. This cuftom of having field prayers has been found fo encouraging and ufeful, that many of the Englifh planters in Grenada, on their becoming owners of French flaves, kept it up on their plantations; yet fome of thefe would have mocked and fneered at the practice, if propofed in their own iflands. In the French colonies even in their towns, there is hardly

---

* Though the French government has cared thus humanely for flaves, though the manners and circumftances of the French planters peculiarly favour their good treatment; yet fince the temper of the mafter muft ftill have great influence on the condition of the flave, this will not prevent, nor can we wonder, when we find, among the French, particular acts oppreffive, and particular owners cruel. But in a vigorous government, fuch as is that of France, thefe acts cannot be frequent, nor thefe men numerous. On the other hand, we muft acknowledge, that the free principles of our conftitution counteract many of the ill effects of our fcandalous neglect of the police of our colonies; and that the tyrannical nature of the French government prevents the French from reaping the full effects of this their benevolent attention to the claims of humanity. Had we governors and other officers as difinterefted as the French, and acting under the like benevolent inftruc-tions, the difference would be highly in our favour; and had the French governors the fame principles to guide them as we have, the French colonifts would enjoy a great acceffion of political happinefs.

occafion

occafion for a lock to fecure goods, or ftore-houfes. In our colonies, no door, or lock, is a fufficient fecurity for any thing which a flave can carry away. In Grenada, they have long bitterly complained, that fince Englifh flaves came among them, they can keep nothing fafe from being purloined, and that even the ho-nefty of their own old flaves has been greatly debauched.

SECT. VI.

Mafter and Slave in the Britifh Colonies.

TO purfue the preceding obfervations, which candour obliged us to make in favour of our rivals, we muft acknowledge, that an Englifh flave has nothing to check him in ill doing, but the fears of the whip, and that is a weak reftraint on a ftarving, craving appetite. The French flave is placed above the folicitations of hunger ; and refpecting his behaviour, has, to the dread of pain, fuperadded, as a guide, the hopes and fears of religion, and the approba-bation and difpleafure of his prieft. The French, in the treatment of their flaves, regard the fuggeftions of humanity, and enforce its dictates by their laws. The Englifh have not paid the leaft attention to enforce by a law either humanity or juftice, as thefe may refpect their flaves. Many are the reftrictions, and fevere

are

are the punifhments, to which our flaves are
fubjeƈed. But if you except a law, that Governor Leake got enaƈted in Nevis, to diflin-
guifh petty larceny in flaves from felony; and
a law in Grenada and Jamaica, that obligeth
maflers to allot to their flaves a certain portion
of land for the growth of provifions; and one
in this laft ifland, that grants them Saturday
afternoon for the culture of it; I recolleƈt not
a fingle claufe in all our colony aƈts, (and I
perufed the feveral codes with the view of remarking fuch) enaƈted to fecure to them the
leaft humane treatment, or to fave them from
the capricious cruelty of an ignorant, unprin-
cipled mafter, or a morofe, unfeeling overfeer.
Nay a horfe, a cow, or a fheep, is much better proteƈted with us by the law, than a poor
flave. For thefe, if found in a trefpafs, are
not to be injured, but fecured for their owners; while a half ftarved negroe, may, for
breaking a fingle cane, which probably he himfelf has planted, be hacked to pieces with a
cutlas; even though, perhaps, he be incapable
of refiflance, or of running away from the
watchman, who finds him in the faƈt. Nay,
we have men among us, who dare boaft of
their giving orders to their watchmen, not to
bring home any flave that they find breaking
of canes, but, as they call it, to *hide* them,
that is to *kill*, and bury them. And, accordingly,

ingly, every now-and-then, fome poor wretch
is miffed, and fome lacerated carcafe is difcovered.

Our countrymen are left, each to be guided
by his own changeable temper, and to be influenced by a femblance of felf-intereft; nor
have they any tie on them, in their behaviour
to the wretches under them, but this 'intereft,
often ill underftood; in fome perhaps there
may be a defire after a reputation for humanity, too frequently little guided by fentiment;
in a few benevolence directed by confcience.
Slaves are efteemed among us the intire property of their mafters, and as having, diftinct
from him, no right or intereft of their own.
And our conftitution has fuch an exceffive bias
to perfonal liberty, that in contradiction to the
maxims of every well ordered ftate, it cannot,
or will not, meddle with private behaviour.
Hence that want of energy, vigour, and even
propriety in every department of our police.
Many actions pafs daily unnoticed among us,
that would have degraded the higheft fenator of
Rome into one of the loweft tribes. Society
profeffes to direct the actions of individuals to
the greateft public good; a purpofe to which
all private intereft and gratification fhould conftantly be made to give place. Hence the true
fecret of police, after having fecured the lives,

liberties,

liberties, and properties of the citizens, is to turn the conduct and induftry of individuals to public profit, confidering the ftate as one whole, and leaving private peifons, each to find his own particular happinefs in public profperity, checking every appearance of a wayward difpofition, that may make the man injurious to his neighbour, or unprofitable to his country. What a field do the Britifh territories offer for fuch a plan of police?

Indeed, with this view before us, our boafted conftitution prefents only an uncultivated wild. How much remains undone in the various departments of commerce, of rural economy, roads, rivers, commons, government of towns, perfection of ftaple commodities, exclufive privileges, and the like? In the cafe of which we treat, the conftitution lays no claim to the flave, but confines its attention to the intercourfe of freemen, leaving citizens at liberty, as mafters, to difpofe of, and treat their flaves, with the fame indifference, if they pleafe, with the fame unfeeling wantonnefs, which without controul they may exercife on their cattle.

While we reflect on the ftate of flavery in our colonies, among the freeft people in the world, and extend our views to the like inftances

ftances in hiftory, it becomes a mournful, an humiliating confideration in human nature, to find that thofe men and nations, whom liberty hath exalted, and who, therefore, ought to regard it tenderly in others, are conftantly for reftraining its bleffings within their own little circle, and delight more in augmenting the train of their dependents, than in adding to the rank of fellow citizens, or in diffufing the bene-fits of freedom among their neighbours. Every where, in every age, the chain of flavery has been fafhioned, and applied by the hand of liberty. Every ancient, every modern ftate gives fhameful evidence of the truth, from the mock manumiffion of the Greeks, by the Roman Flaminius, to the oppreffed ftate of the Dutch barrier, and their Eaft Indian fettle-ments, begun while they themfelves were ftrug-gling for freedom. *

* The Athenians never admitted ftrangers to the privilege of citizenfhip; Hercules, and one or two more, being the only foreigners indulged with it. This accounts for the fhort period of their once fplendid maritime empire. It is true the Romans fucceffively admitted their neighbours, accord-ing to their vicinity, to the privilege of citizens; but they acted from no generous principle. They increafed the num-ber of tyrants, in proportion as their conquefts added new flaves to be kept in fubjection by them. Of this the focial war is an undoubted proof. Yet this conduct, though fpring-ing from unworthy motives, was followed with the beft effects, and gave ftability to a ftate, that conqueft otherwife might have ruined.

It

It will perhaps be alleged, that this inconfiderate treatment of flaves in our colonies may,
as is generally fuppofed in Britain, be the effect
of the illiberal turn of the colonifts, accuftomed from their infancy to trifle with the
feelings, and fmile at the miferies, of wretches
born to be the drudges of their avarice, and
flaves of their caprice. . But it is to be remarked, that adventurers from Europe are univerfally more cruel and morofe towards flaves,
than Creoles, or native Weft-Indians. Indeed,
whatever I fhall have to fay of the conduct
of individuals towards flaves, and the inattention of mafters towards their claims, may
be applied with more juftice to the new fet-
tlers, than to the natives. Often attachment
will fecure from thefe laft good ufage, while
the flave has no hold on the others; nay, probably is degraded by over-weening European
pride, into a ftate differing but in name from
brutal, by a treatment lefs generous, lefs confiderate, than a horfe or an ox receives from
them. Oppreffion makes the wretches ftupid,
and their ftupidity becomes their crime, and
provokes their farther punifhment. In particular, in the colony from which the following
obfervations are chiefly drawn, fo great is the
proportion of Europeans in all its active ftations, that the character of the community
muft be taken from them, not from the natives.

And

And when one confiders how thefe adventurers are ufually collected, how often the refufe of each man's connections, of every trade, and every profeffion, are thronged in upon them, much fentiment, morality, or religion, cannot well be expected to be found within the circle of their influence. This muft ferve as an apology for any thing feemingly fevere, that may appear in the profecution of the fubject; to which we now return. *

The difcipline of a fugar plantation is as exact as that of a regiment: at four o'clock in the morning the plantation bell rings to call the flaves into the field. Their work is to manure, dig, and hoe, plow the ground, to plant, weed, and cut the cane, to bring it to the mill, to have the juice expreffed and boiled into fugar. About nine o'clock, they have half an hour for breakfaft, which they take in the field. Again they fall to work, and, according to the cuftom of the plantation, continue until eleven o'clock, or noon ; the bell then rings, and

* We muft not confound every European fettler in the above cenfure; fentiment, and benevolence, refined by education, influence feveral fuch within the author's acquaintance. Indeed, whatever there is generally amifs in the conduct of mafters to their flaves, arifes not fo much from any particular depravity in them as men, as from the arbitrary unnatural relation that exifts between them and their wretched dependents; the effects of which, neither fentiment nor morality can at all times prevent.

and the flaves are difperfed in the neighbourhood, to pick up about the fences, in the mountains, and fallow or wafte grounds, natural grafs 'and weeds for the horfes and cattle. The time allotted for this branch of work, and preparation for dinner, varies from an hour and an half, to near three hours. In colleɗing pile by pile their little bundles of grafs, the flaves of low land plantations, frequently burnt up by the fun, muft wander in their neighbours grounds, perhaps more than two miles from home. In their return, often fome lazy fellow, of the intermediate plantation, with the view of faving himfelf the trouble of picking his own grafs, feizes on them, and pretends to infift on carrying them to his mafter, for picking grafs, or being found in his grounds ; a crime that forfeits the bundle, and fubjeɗs the offender to twenty lafhes of a long cart whip, of twifted leather thongs. The wretch, rather than be carried to judgment in another man's plantation, is fain to efcape with the lofs of his bundle, and often to put up quietly with a good drubbing from the robber into the bargain. The hour of delivering in his grafs, and renewing his tafk, approaches, while hunger importunately folicits him to remember its call ; but he muft renew the irkfome toil, and fearch out fome green, fhady, unfrequented fpot, from which to repair his lofs.

At

At one, or in fome plantations, at two o'clock, the bell fummons them to deliver in the tale of their grafs, and affemble to their field work. If the overfeer thinks their bundles too fmall, or if they come too late with them, they are punifhed with a number of ftripes from four to ten. Some mafters, under a fit of carefulnefs for their cattle, have gone as far as fifty ftripes, which effectually difable the culprit for weeks. If a flave has no grafs to deliver in, he keeps away out of fear, fkulks about in the mountains, and is abfent from his work often for months ; an aggravation of his crime, which, when he is caught, he is made to remember.

About half an hour before fun fet, they may be found fcattered again over the land, like the Ifraelites in Egypt, to cull, blade by blade, from among the weeds, their fcanty parcels of grafs. About feven o'clock in the evening, or later, according to the feafon of the year, when the overfeer can find leifure, they are called over by lift, to deliver in their fecond bundles of grafs ; and the fame punifhment, as at noon, is inflicted on the delinquents. They then feparate, to pick up, in their way to their huts, (if they have not done it, as they generally do, while gathering grafs) a little brufh wood, or dry cow-dung, to prepare fome fimple mefs for fupper, and to-morrow's breakfaft. This em-
ploys

ploys them till near midnight, and then they go to fleep, till the bell calls them in the morning.

This picking of grafs, as it is fitly called, often in a fevere drought, when it is to be found only in the receffes of the mountain, thus thruft in by the by into the hour of wearinefs and reft, is the greateft hardfhip that a flave endures, and the moft frequent caufe of his running away, or abfenting himfelf from his work ; which not only fubjects him to frequent punifhment, but actually renders him unprofitable, worthlefs, and deferving of punifhment. He can neither refrefh, or indulge his wearied body. He is fubjected by it to injury. He is placed in the jaws of trefpafs, and unavoidably made obnoxious to oppreffion, and ftripes. And yet a few acres of land, in proportion to the extent of the plantation, allotted for artificial grafs, and a few weakly flaves feparated from the work, would take away the neceffity of providing for cattle in this haraffing fcanty manner.

This grafs, except fuch part of it as is referved for the ftable horfes, procured by fo much toil, and forced out of the flave by fuch repeated punifhment, under pretence of feeding the cattle and mules, is fpread abroad under their feet, on a fermenting inclofed dung heap, called a pen. There a very confiderable part is loft to every purpofe of nourifhment, by being

trampled

trampled under the beafts feet ; where mixing with dung and urine, it ferments, corrupts, and with its fuffocating fteams in that fultry climate, inftead of fupplying them with vigour, fills them with difeafe ; as if Providence meant to revenge the oppreffion of the flave, in being forced to drudge thus for it, by infpiring the mafter with a fpirit of abfurdity, in his manner of ufing it. *

The work here mentioned, is confidered as the field duty of flaves, that may be infifted on without reproach to the manager, of unufual feverity,

* This pen is an inclofure, perhaps of fixty by eighty feet, in which, from thirty to fifty cattle and mules are kept and fed. The decayed leaves, and offals of the fugar cane, are from time to time thrown in for litter. Their provender is fpread over it, and being mixed with urine, dung, and rain, becomes a fermenting mafs, which is emptied once, and in fome plantations, twice a year. The difeafe generally fatal to mules, feems to be of the nature of a putrid infectious fever, which, if it does not arife from, is at leaft heightened by, this abfurd manner of feeding. The cattle being often ftaked out in the fallow grounds, are not fo conftantly expofed to thefe noxious fteams.

Though a planter will readily pay 30l. fterling for a good mule, or a bull, and though chiefly from this fcanty abfurd method of feeding them, he be obliged to renew his expence from year to year : yet will he not allow a few acres for arti-ficial grafs, nor even a ftall, a manger, or a clean fpot, to fave their fmall pittance of provender from filth, or to feed them apart from the foul exhalations of a dung heap, in its moft un-wholefome ftate. There have been inftances of pens burfting out into a fmouldering flame, while the cattle were feeding on them.

feverity, and which the white and black overfeers ftand over them to fee executed; the
tranfgreffion againft which, is quickly followed with the fmart of the cart whip. This
inftrument, in the hands of a fkilful driver, cuts
out flakes of fkin and flefh with every ftroke;
and the wretch, in this mangled condition, is
turned out to work in dry or wet weather,
which laft, now and then, brings on the cramp,
and ends his fufferings and flavery together.

In crop-time, which may be when reckoned
altogether on a plantation, from five to fix
months; the cane tops, by fupplying the cattle
with food, gives the flaves fome little relaxation
in picking grafs. But fome pretendedly induftrious planters, men of much buftle, and no
method, will, efpecially in moon-light, keep
their people till ten o'clock at night, carrying
wowra, the decayed leaves of the cane, to boil
off the cane juice. A confiderable number of
flaves is kept to attend in turn the mill and
boiling houfe all night. They fleep over their
work; the fugar is ill tempered, burnt in the
boiler, and improperly ftruck; while the mill
every now-and-then grinds off an hand, or an
arm, of thofe drowfy worn down creatures that
feed it. Still the procefs of making fugar is
carried on in many plantations, for months,
without any other interruption, than during
fome part of day light on Sundays. In fome
                                    plantations

plantations it is the cuſtom, during crop-time, to keep the whole gang employed as above, from morning to night, and alternately one half throughout the night, to ſupply the mill with canes, and the boiling houſe with wowra.

This labour is more or leſs moderated, in proportion to the method and good ſenſe of the manager. In ſome plantations the young children and worn-out ſlaves are ſet apart to pick graſs, and bring cane tops from the field for the cattle, and do no other work. Sometimes the field gangs bring both their bundles of graſs at once, being allowed for that purpoſe a little extra time, during the meridian heat; which ſaves them an unneceſſary repetition of wandering in the evening three or four miles to ſearch for it, and enables the manager to employ the cool part of the afternoon in the common labour of the plantation. Sometimes they are diſmiſſed for graſs before the uſual hour; or if they be hoe-ploughing land, frequently none is required from them. In ſome plantations, they are not puniſhed for coming late into the field, if they appear there about ſun-riſe. In moſt well-ordered plantations, they leave off grinding and boiling before midnight, and begin not again till about dawn: it having been found, that the quantity of ſugar made in the night, is not in proportion to the time; that it not only ſuffers in quality, but alſo lies open to pilferage; and
that

that the mules, particularly the moſt tractable, and eaſily harneſſed, are injured by being worked indiſcriminately, in the dark, out of their turn; another valuable conſequence, this of their being confuſedly huddled together in that incloſed dung-heap, the pen: for the danger of grinding off a drowſy negroe's arm, or haraſſing him to death, is a conſideration which, without theſe other circumſtances, would hardly interrupt the grand work of ſugar-making.

Every plantation contains little ſkirts, and portions of broken land, unfit for the cultivation of ſugar. Theſe are uſually divided among the ſlaves for the growth of proviſions; but where the maſter is inattentive, a few of the principal negroes often ſeize on, and appropriate to them-ſelves, the poſſeſſions of the reſt, and make the ſimpler ſort labour for them; and many are ſo lazy, that nothing but the whip, and the pre-ſence of the overſeer, can make them work, even for themſelves. There is ſuch a ready market for all the little articles which theſe ſpots produce, that the induſtrious ſlaves of a few, though but a few, plantations ſituated near the mountains, where the weather is ſeaſonable and favours the growth of vegetables, maintain themſelves in clothes and food, tolerably well, by the ſale of their various fruits, with little other immediate aid from their maſter, beſides a weekly allowance of herrings. But, in far the

greater

greater number of plantations, the quantity of provifions, or marketable vegetables, is uncertain and trifling; and neceffity and hunger will not permit the wretches, to leave them in the ground to ripen fufficiently. Hence many difeafes and ruined conftitutions, from this fcanty, rude, ill-prepared food, ufed among them.

Formerly, before we became fuch accurate planters, and before luxury had rapacioufly converted every little nook of land into fugar, the flaves had a field or two of the fallow cane-land yearly divided among them, for a crop of yams, peafe, and potatoes; and a field of the beft cane-land was annually put in yams, to be referved for their weekly allowance. When our late North American brethren were pleafed to threaten our fugar iflands with famine, this cuftom began again to be renewed, and with fuch fuccefs as might have encouraged them, never, in time to come, to have made themfelves as dependent on North America as formerly for their daily bread.

Some mafters, now-and-then, give their flaves Saturday afternoon, out of crop-time, to till their fpots of ground; fometimes will turn in the whole gang among them to weed and put them in order, under the direction of the overfeer. But, in general, *the culture of their private patches, and the picking of grafs for their*

their cattle, are their employments on Sunday. In
the low lands thefe provifion fpots are hardly
ufeful fix months in twelve, from the ufual
drinefs of the weather.   Added to the produce
of their own provifion lands, and the cafualty
of a fallow field, the flaves have a weekly
allowance of grain, varying in different plantations, from one to three pounds, under the
nominal meafure of from two to eight pints.
A few plantations go near to five pounds ; one
or two as far as fix. They have alfo from
three to eight herrings a week. In general,
they are far from being well or plentifully fed.*

They

---

* The practice of turning all our lands to the growth of
the fugar cane, and neglecting the culture of provifions for
the flaves, and of artificial grafs for the cattle, has lately
arifen equally from the demands of extravagance in our abfent
planters, and of poverty in thofe on the fpot. Sugar, fugar,
is the inceffant cry of luxury, and of debt. To increafe the
quantity of this commodity, gardens of half an acre have
been grubbed up ; and that little patch, which he had ufed to
till for his own peafe, or caffava, has the flave been made to
dig for the reception of his mafter's fugar cane. Nor has the
little fkirt of pafture, or half rood of artificial grafs, been
more fpared in this univerfal facrifice to would-be greainefs ;
while the poor flave muft attempt to make up for this, and
every other want but his own, by exertions taken from the
hour of wearinefs and hunger. Hence the annual expence of
plantations, within lefs than thirty years, has been more than
doubled. Hence the fending of two or three extra cafks of
fugar to market has been attended with an expence of hundreds of pounds in provifions to flaves, in oats to horfes,
and in keeping up the ftock of flaves and cattle, worn out,
before

They have an yearly allowarce of two or three yards of coarfe woollen cloth, called bamboo, to which fometimes is added for the men a woollen cap, for the women a handkerchief, and perhaps a few yards of Ofnaburghs. At Chriftmas three holidays are pretended to be given them; but generally Sunday is foifted in for one, and now and then half of Chriftmas-day muft be employed by them in digging yams for their allowance, and in receiving it afterwards, with a pound or two of falt-fifh, or a fcrap of coarfe Irifh beef. In Jamaica they have alfo two holidays at Eafter, and two at Whitfuntide.

Their huts are framed of ifland timber, cut by each man for himfelf in the mountains, and carried down by him and his wife on Sundays. Sometimes the owner will fupply a board or two to make a door or window fhutter, but, in general, fuch materials are ftolen; nails and hinges

---

before their time, by indifcreet extraordinary efforts, and a fcanty allowance. The peculiar fertility of St. Chriftopher's has the moft baneful effects. It enables the greateft part of its proprietors to live in England; where, infenfible of the fufferings of their flaves, they think and dream of nothing but fugar, fugar; to which, in confequence, every fpot of land is condemned. Hence grafs is procured there with more difficulty, and the flaves are more fcantily fed, than in the other iflands; and the managers are obliged to keep them up to their utmoft poffible exertion to preferve their employment.

·hinges are either ftolèn or bought from thofe who have ftolen them. This often happens on a plantation where perhaps a thoufand pounds fterling have been expended on a ftable for a fet of Englifh horfes. Indeed Englifh horfes are the leaft neceffary, yet beft attended, beft ferved, beft lodged, and moft expenfively kept, animals poffeffed by a fugar planter.

Negroes bred to mechanic employments, to fugar boiling, and the like, and fome domeftic flaves, fare much better than thofe who work in the field. They have opportunities of retaliating on their mafter for his penurious treatment of them, by purloining from him; and they often fupply themfelves with neceffaries by little ufeful jobs in their feveral trades. Slaves in the neighbourhood of the towns drive alfo a confiderable trade with the inhabitants for grafs and cane tops for feeding their horfes.

A furgeon is generally employed by the year to attend the fick flaves. His allowance per head varies from fourteen-pence to three fhillings; in a few inftances it rifes to three fhillings and fix-pence fterling, befides being paid for amputations. Some frugal planters truft to their own fkill, and James's powder, and Ward's pill; and, then, for the moft part, a furgeon is only called in to pronounce them

paft

paſt recovery. The food of the ſick is often muſty, indigeſtible horſe beans, ſometimes maize, flour, or rice ; ſometimes, as a dainty, brown biſcuit. On ſome plantations, the ma-- nager is allowed to get, now-and-then, a fowl, or a kid to make ſoup for them. Sometimes the owner ſends the manager a caſk of wine, a few glaſſes of which are ſuppoſed to be for the uſe of the ſick. Where the manager is a married man, the ſick often have a meſs from his table, and caudle, tea, and other comfort- able ſlops ; and his wife ſuperintends the con- duct of the nurſe, and ſees that the pregnant and lying-in women be properly taken care of. But the cuſtom of employing married men on plantations is wearing faſt out. Though mar- ried managers alone can take proper care of the ſick, though they ſtay more conſtantly at home, and have numberleſs other advantages over ſingle men, in point of character, faithfulneſs, and application ; yet planters have determined it to be better to employ perhaps a diſſipated, careleſs, unfeeling young man, or a grovelling, laſcivious, old batchelor (each with his half ſcore of black or mulattoe pilfering harlots, who, at their will, ſelect for him, from among the ſlaves, the objects of his favour or hatred) rather than allow a married woman to be entertained on the plantation.* In

* The pretence of this encouragement given to profligacy, is, that a family requires more attendants, and conſumes more ſugar

In the year 1774, or before the American war, the feveral articles that a flave had annually returned to him out of his labour, were, in too many plantations, within the following proportion. In others, his allowance of food confiderably exceeded what is here mentioned :

fugar than a fingle man; but the contrary is the fact in a very high degree; and there is not in the fingle man the attention, and perfevering care of a fenfible woman, (fuch, in an highly ufeful degree, is almoft every manager's wife whom I know) in things within her province, which, even, were the affertion true, would more than balance the account.

I mean not to comprehend every fingle man in the full extent of this cenfures. Some fhew the wretches under them every mark of attention that their own folitary ftate leaves in their power. But all muft pafs through the hands of fome inconfiderate boy overfeer, or fome unfeeling black or mulattoe concubine. And where the fingle man is a gadding, goffipping reveller, (a character fometimes to be met with) inconceivable are the miferies to which the flaves are fubjected. The neceffaries, where any are allotted for the fick, (and heaven knows, on the beft plantations, they are trivial enough!) are devoured as a morfel, by that legion of harlots and their children, with which the plantation abounds. Often, while the manager is feafting abroad, carelefs and ignorant of what has happened, fome haplefs wretch among the flaves is taken ill, and unnoticed, unpitied, dies, without even the poor comfort of a furgeon, in his laft moments, to fay, " It is now too late." When the unripe female flave has become the new object of the manager's attachment, fhe becomes an object of envy to the more experienced damesthat have gone before her, and muft think herfelf lucky, if fhe pays not with her life the forfeit of her youthful attractions. In fhort, in the cafe fuppofed, fhamelefs profligacy ufurps the place of decency, fympathy, morality, and religion; and headlong unthinking luft alone produces all the wafting effects of difhonefty, cruelty, and oppreffion.

Annual

	£.	s.	d.
Annual allowance of rice, flour, maize, beans, or other grain,	0	12	0
Ditto of herrings, and his fifh, or fcrap of falt beef, at Chriftmas,	0	8	0
Ditto clothing, - - - - - -	0	3	6
Surgeon, quack medicines, and extraordinary neceffaries when fick,	0	2	6
Whole annual allowance -	1	6	0

The ordinary punifhments of flaves, for the common crimes of negleﬀ, abfence from work, eating the fugar cane, theft, are cart whipping, beating with a ftick, fometimes to the breaking of bones, the chain, an iron crook about the neck, a large iron pudding or ring about the ancle, and confinement in the dungeon. There have been inftances of flitting of ears, breaking of limbs, fo as to make amputation neceffary, beating out of eyes, and caftration; but they feldom happen, efpecially of late years, and though they bring no lafting difgrace on the perpetrator, have, for fome time paft, been generally mentioned with indignation. It is yet true, that the unfeeling application of the ordinary punifhments ruins the conftitution, and fhortens the life of many a poor wretch.*

To

---

* In a certain colony, no lefs than two chief judges within thefe thirty years, have been celebrated for cutting off or mafhing

To avoid any misconstruction, I must here observe, that the labour, the diet, the punishments, in short, the general treatment of slaves, depend on the character of the owner or manager; and that in some particular plantations (the grievance of picking grass, and the circumstance of their being so long as sixteen hours out of the twenty-four under the lash of the whip, excepted) they enjoy as much ease and indulgence as are compatible with their present state of ignorance and dependence, and the accurate methodical cultivation of a sugar plantation. But this case and this indulgence, though due from all masters to all slaves, are not deemed matter of right, but of kindness or favour; and too many are set over them, who want both humanity and discretion to see either the obligation or advantage of such treatment; too many who are too lazy to consult any principle but present caprice in their conduct towards them. I have heard managers boast of

mashing (so as to make amputation necessary) the limbs of their slaves. In one case a surgeon was called in to operate; but he answered, he was not obliged to be the instrument of another man's cruelty. His honour had it then performed by a cooper's adze, and the wretch was left to bleed to death, without attention, or dressing. When he became convulsed, in the agonies of death, the surgeon was again hastily sent for, and came in time to pronounce him dead. People stared at the recital, but made no enquiry for blood. In the other case the limb was mashed with a sledge hammer, and then it was amputated by a surgeon, and the maimed wretch lived some years.

not

not having ordered twelve ftripes in twelve months among 120 flaves. There are alfo managers who may boaft, and there have been fome who have boafted, of having given, every now-and-then, what they call a cool hundred for the flighteft offences. Yet, were this laft even a folitary chara&er, in a community, he ought to be an obje& of police, and be compelled to revere the claims of human nature.

We cannot pafs over in filence the ufual treatment of pregnant women and nurfes. In almoft every plantation they are fond of placing every negroe who can wield an hoe in the field gang; fo fond, that hardly any remonftrance from the furgeon can, in many cafes, fave a poor difeafed wretch from the labour; though, if method prevailed, work may be found on the plantation equally neceffary and proportioned to every various degree of ability; and though one or two days attempts in the field be fure to lay them up in the hofpital for weeks.

At this work are pregnant women often kept during the laft months of their pregnancy, and hence fuffer many an abortion; which fome managers are unfeeling enough to exprefs their

E 2 joy

joy at, becaufe the woman, on recovery, having no child to care for, will have no pretence
for indulgence.

If, after all, fhe carries her burden the full
time, fhe muft be delivered in a dark, damp,
fmoky hut, perhaps without a rag in which
to wrap her child, except the manager has a
wife to fympathize with her wants. Hence the
frequent lofs of negroe children by cramp and
convulfions within the month. A lying-in woman is allowed three, in fome plantations four
weeks for recovery. She then takes the field
with her child, and hoe or bill. The infant
is placed in the furrow, near her, generally
expofed naked, or almoft naked, to the fun and
rain, on a kid fkin, or fuch rags as fhe can
procure. Some very few people give nurfes
an extra allowance. In general, no other attention is paid to their condition, except perhaps to excufe them from the picking of grafs.

Though flaves be now raifed to a price that
few old fettled plantations can afford to give,
yet this is all the care taken in moft of them
to raife a young generation; while Creoles or
native Weft Indian negroes are univerfally acknowledged to be more hardy, diligent, and
trufty than Africans. Managers, to whofe care
plantations are left, hold their places, as we
have obferved, by fo precarious a tenure, that
they

they too often confine their views to the making of the greateſt preſent exertion that is poſſible, (which, indeed, their employers preſs
them to do) without looking forward to what
may happen fifteen years hence *.

. - S E C T.

* Under the impreſſion of this negligence, let me propoſe
the remedy. Let two rooms be added to the hoſpital, one for
the reception of lying-in women, the other for the ſucking
children, while their mothers are at work. The whole ſhould
be placed ſo as to be convenient for the inſpection of the
manager's wife, whom we eſteem to be as neceſſary a perſon
on a plantation as the manager himſelf; and who, on moſt
plantations, may have ſufficient employment in taking care
of the keys in her huſband's abſence on buſineſs, or at courts,
(many overſeers not being truſt-worthy) to ſee the ſickly negroes
fed, the infants properly taken care of, and the nurſe do her
duty in the hoſpital. For theſe and the like offices, in St.
Croix, it is uſual to give her a ſalary, diſtinct from her huſband. Let two elderly handy women be choſen to attend the
children, keep them clean, and feed them with ſpoon-meat.
For the firſt ſix months, nurſes ſhould be kept at moderate
labour near the hoſpital, to be at hand to ſuckle their children, from time to time. After that period, they may go
through the ordinary work of the plantation, except the picking of graſs. They ſhould have an extraordinary allowance of
food both in quantity and quality. Every healthy child, preſented to the maſter weaned, ſhould intitle the mother to a
complete ſuit of clothes. Every woman, that has three children at work in the field, ſhould be excuſed all field work.

We have ſeveral plantations, where by care and mild
treatment, and a judicious, or caſually juſt proportion between the ſexes at firſt, the ſlaves increaſe from the births;
and this might be the caſe in all, if the dictates of prudence
and humanity were obeyed. To give an inſtance in point:
there are two plantations, bordering on each other, of nearly
the ſame extent. About twenty years ago they were nearly
equally

SECT. VII.

Mafter and Slave in particular Inftances.

I T has been obferved, that there is no law in the colonies to reftrain the ill-behaviour or cruelty of a mafter to his flave. It is not meant to be infinuated from this, that the want of laws to fecure good treatment to them expofeth them to all the ill ufage, that may be fuppofed naturally to arife from fuch neglect. The humanity of many mafters more than fupplies the want of laws in every other refpect, but that of improvement ; the attachment of others has in them a like effect. In fome cafes, good fenfe, a regard for their reputation, and a well informed conviction of their intereft, induce men to treat their flaves with difcretion and humanity. The flaves of many a planter poffefs advantages beyond what the labourer even in Britain enjoys.

It

equally ftocked with flaves: on the one the allowance has been more plentiful, and the managers have been more confiderate than on the other. Here the flaves are ftrong, hearty, and increafed from the births. The other manager boafts of his pinching and faving : and that plantation requires an almoft annual fupply of eight or ten negroes to keep up the ftock. And, till lately, that he, through laz'nefs, and abfolute neglect of his employer's intereft, as he underftood it, has relaxed in his difcipline, the flaves were a ftarving heartlefs crew. Indeed, at this time, none were left but fuch whofe natural ftrength of conftitution ftood proof againft excefs of labour, feverity of punifhment, and the laft tolerable degree of famine.

It is true the flave cannnot hope, as the other may, to raife himfelf, or his children above their prefent condition; or by his induftry to put himfelf or them on a footing with his mafter; a fpur to exertion and emulation that muft ever diftinguifh and ennoble freedom: yet his work, all but that vile picking of grafs, which in St. Chriftopher's is an intolerable burden, is in general eafier; his life paffes more happily on, and he entertains no anxious thoughts about his expences when fick, or his maintenance when old. Slaves chiefly fuffer, where they are the property of an ignorant, low-minded, narrow-hearted wretch, or of one indigent and involved, or of a man who makes a figure beyond his income in England, or when they are fubmitted to fome raw lad, or untaught unfeeling manager or overfeer. And men in fuch circumftances, and of fuch difpofitions, are to be found in too great a proportion in every community, to have abandoned to their ignorance, their cruelty, prejudice, parfimony, or felfifhnefs, fo many thoufands of their fellow-creatures as are really fubjected to them in our colonies.

I have now in contemplation before me, a planter, who conceives himfelf to be a confcientious man. This man fells every year fugar and rum to the amount of 10,000 l. or 15,000 l. fterling, befides duties and freight; the produce
of

of his flaves labour, in number above 500. Though his lands have no particular advantages of provifion grounds above his neighbours, and though he never was remarkable for allowing them any extraordinary time to work fuch ground, if it had been allotted to them, nay, is notorious for keeping them drawling on at work under the eye of his drivers and overfeers, from earlieft dawn to midnight, from month to month, without refpite or relaxation; yet it is only of late years, that he has afforded them any thing above fix herrings a week, and thofe not very regularly fupplied. His manager, indeed, ufed to fteal, now-and-then, from his horfes, a bufhel or two of beans to divide among the moft emaciated flaves; but it was not the cuftom of the plantation to give them any allowance of food. Some years ago, his attornies took the opportunity of his making a voyage to England, to give his flaves an allowance of grain which has fince been continued, and has gradually been raifed from a fcanty pound per week to nearly the common allowance of fix nominal pints, that may weigh about two pounds and an half. Indeed, fuch was this man's original prejudice againft feeding his negroes, and fo unable were they, without feeding, to exift in a ftate capable of labour, that, greatly to the leffening of his income, it was his cuftom to keep on making fugar, almoft throughout the whole year, in a

lifelefs,

lifelefs, inactive manner, in order that his flaves
might have fome fubfiftence from the cane juice.
Before the period of which we fpeak, flaves
had much more provifion ground allotted to
them, and, being lefs hurried by the overfeers,
were better able to cultivate. When luxury
came in, like a torrent, among the planters, and
feized with violence on the flaves little fpots,
and demanded the whole of their time, not leaving even to fleep its due, the neceffity of providing other food for them from foreign parts
was but flowly perceived, and thoufands had pe-
rifhed before the lofs was traced to its proper
caufe; and this man, of whom we write, was
one of the laft who was convinced that his flaves
muft be fed, if work was to be expected from
them. Now can it be affirmed, that fuch a perfon would not have reaped an advantage from a
law that fhould have directed him how to feed
his flaves, or that flaves belonging to fuch a man
would not have been happier in themfelves,
more profitable to their owner, and better and
more ufeful members of the ftate, if they could
have claimed the benefit of a law, I will not
fay to vindicate for them the common rights of
humanity, but to fecure to them the full exertion of their animal powers. And may we not
add, that men fo ufeful to fociety in their mif-
managed ftate, and capable of being rendered
infinitely more profitable, have demands on fo-

E 5   ciety

ciety for much better entertainment than a bit
of falted herring, or a little raw cane juice?

And yet, had fuch planters as we have been
fpeaking of the fenfe to difcern it, wifdom would
teach them a more liberal plan of policy, and
make the dictates of humanity, or even of prudence alone, ftand in ftead of a thoufand laws.
A gentleman, who lately died here, gave his
flaves nearly double the proportion of food that
is given by many, who value themfelves on feeding them very high; and he frequently faid,
that, could he afford it, he would increafe their
allowance ftill further. He parcelled out to
them a larger proportion of his ufeful ground
than moft of his neighbours, for the cultivation
of their roots and vegetables, and it lay more
convenient for tillage. His flaves had all fome
little property, a hog, a goat, a trifle of money
made by the fale of the produce of their little
gardens; or of their weekly allowance of food;
and they were all able to keep themfelves decently clothed. He enlarged the gang to fuch a
number, as not to be under the neceflity of working them beyond their ftrength, or at unfeafon-
able hours. In wet weather, he contrived to
employ them near the works for the benefit of
fhelter; and they all had comfortable huts to receive them after the labour of the day. He allowed them to exchange their provifions for money,

ney, or any other fpecies of food more agreeable
to them, and it was to enable them to indulge
their tafte for variety, that he wifhed to increafe an allowance, otherwife fufficient for
them. He feemed to have hit the medium between governing too much and too little: his
people were always ready at command; but
they had the full power of themfelves and their
time, when the plantation work did not employ
them.

When he left off the purchafing of new flaves,
he poffeffed about one hundred and fixty. In
four years they were increafed from the births
to one hundred and eighty. In *eight years* he
had loft by old age and chronic complaints about
ten, and a few more by the natural fmall-pox,
who, when the others were inoculated, were
paffed over, on the fuppofition of their having
formerly had the difeafe. Some few infants
were, I believe, alfo loft within the month;
and the proportion of breeding women was
fmall. The above is not the common proportion of deaths in any place. It is not an unufual thing on the fame ifland to lofe *in one year*
out of fuch a number, *ten, twelve,* nay, as far as
twenty, by fevers, fluxes, dropfies, the effect of
too much work, and too little food and care.
In fome plantations of the like extent, it is neceffary to keep up the gang by an almoft annual
addition

addition of eight or ten new flaves. His whole expence for phyfic, during the three laft years of this period, was within half of the annual allowance ufually paid for fuch a number. Now, if we take into account the labour loft by the ficknefs of thofe numbers that muft be taken ill, where many die, the expence of recruits, and the puny, weakly, inefficient ftate of the whole, where fo much is fuffered from inattention, the difference in point of intereft between difcreet and hard ufage is great in favour of humanity.

Farther, in plantations, where flaves are ill fed, hard worked, and feverely punifhed, it is a circumftance common for a tenth, and even as far as a fourth part of the working flaves, to go off and fkulk in the mountains, fome for months together. The culture of the plantation is interrupted by the lofs of their labour, while they, by lying out in the woods, and learning there to eat dirt or clay, often contract diforders, of which they never recover. This gentleman, in the laft eight years of his life, had only one flave who abfented himfelf two days, on having had fome words with the overfeer, for having debauched one of his wives. Thefe particulars taken together, are not defpicable advantages of fellowfeeling and humanity; and if the like care was extended to the improvement of their minds, they, who were fo well cared

cared for in what refpects the body, might in time be brought to pay fome attention to what concerns the foul.

It is pleafant to record fuch an inftance, and, did I not fear to awaken detraction, I would in order to humble European pride, celebrate him by name, as a Creole of at leaft four defcents, the friend of the author, and a man of more confiderable humanity in private, and more comprehenfive generofity in public life, than (except in one or two cafes more) has ever come within my notice. But this gentleman had chiefly in view the eafe and happinefs of his own flaves : perhaps an example, where profit is the object, may be more convincing. A young man has the care of a confiderable plantation in the neighbourhood : his character depends on its thriving condition, and the profitable returns made to the abfent owner. The flaves, when he took charge of them, were a puny weakly gang, and fewer in number than in other plantations of the fame extent. The plantation is particularly laborious, yet the work is more forward, and better finifhed, the flaves more healthy, the deaths fewer, the crops greater, the rum in an higher proportion, and the fugar better and higher priced, than in the plantations around it.

This

This is the fecret of his management. He
is a flave to method. If once he hath taken
public notice of a trefpafs againft the eftablifhed
difcipline, he never pardons, except when, in
a particular cafe, he obliges the culprit to find
fome reputable fellow-flave, to become fecurity
with him for his good behaviour. He attends
carefully to his own duty, and therefore few under him dare to be negligent; fo that he feldom
has occafion to correct. The trial of all tref-
paffes, and difpenfation of punifhments, are held
in prefence of the gang. The fentence is accompanied with a public explanation of the
fault, and an exhortation to avoid it; and often
the contempt and reproach of the culprit's fellows make the fevereft part of the correction.
If the whole gang has behaved remarkably well,
throughout the week, he diftributes fome little
reward among them, or, if the work permits,
gives them Saturday afternoon to themfelves.
If a flave has been remarkably diligent, he gets
fome money, a bit of beef, or other trifle on
Sunday. Sometimes he affects to difcover remarkable diligence in a lazy flave, and rewards
it as if real, and thus encourages him to exert
himfelf, and excites thofe who defpifed him, ftill
more to out-do him. If two or three behave
remarkably ill, the ufual indulgence or reward is
with-held from the gang. This makes them
become guardians of each other's conduct, and

fear

fear the fcorn and refentment of their companions, more than their mafter's power. He em-
braces every occafion to harangue them on their
duty, and on the advantage of obedience, and
good behaviour; and this cuftom has infenfibly
introduced among them the feeds of fentiment,
and moral diftinction. Their allowance of food
is double to that of plantations where they pretend to give the fame number of pints of grain.
When they hole, or hand plough, the land, they
have an extraordinary allowance of food, and are
indulged with rum and water to drink. The
fick, and their nurfe, are put under his wife's
direction, and any remarkably puny negro is
employed about the houfe and kitchen.

CHAP.

C H A P. II.

The Advancement of Slaves would augment their Social Importance.

IN the preceding chapter, we have contrafted flavery, as it has been variously enforced among different nations, over the unfortunate, with thofe ranks, into which fociety naturally, and profitably, feparates its members. In this laft ftate, we obferve a rule originating in our con-ftitution, by our Creator's will, that leads on each individual from his own fecurity and hap-pinefs, to form the happinefs and fecurity of the community to which he belongs. In the other, the capricious will of individuals is the only law of their dependents, and, without once confult-ing their welfare, concludes all their feelings, and all their deareft interefts. And all mafters, in proportion as they themfelves are free, are, for their mutual profit, confpired together to rivet, and extend the chains of flavery, as far as their power extends.

This unnatural ftate of mankind has, more or lefs, departed from the dictates of humanity, in proportion as the difpofition of mafters, and the views of legiflators, have overlooked or confi-dered

dered the general rights of mankind. The cuftoms and manners of different nations have, in
fome inftances, foftened the lot of miferable
flaves ; in others have encouraged the head-long.
cruelty of mafters. But in the Britifh plantations, the infolence arifing from the keen fenfe
of our own freedom, (and yet why fhould not a
keener fympathy with fuffering humanity operate on our feelings) and the inceffant demands
of luxury, and extravagance, that make themfelves to be heard, and obeyed from the capital
acrofs the vaft atlantic, have there funk human
nature down to the loweft depth of wretchednefs. Hunger, miftruft, oppreffion, ignorance,
produce in the flaves worthleffnefs, and crimes ;
and the avarice and cruelty, that contrived the
faults, exact punifhment for them with as much
effrontery, as if they who made them flaves,
and thereby deprived them of every virtuous
feeling, and every fpur to emulation, were not
anfwerable in their own perfons for the bafe
effects. Do we wifh to form adequate notions
of their mifery ? Let us imagine (and would
heaven it were only imagination !) mafters and
overfeers, with uplifted whips, clanking chains,
and preffing hunger, forcing their forlorn flaves
to commit every horrid crime that virtue fhrinks
at, and with the fame weapons punifhing the
perpetration, not to the extremity indeed that
nature can bear, but till the whole man finks
under them. But to make the reprefentation
complete,

complete, we muſt alſo draw humanity, bleeding over the horrid ſcene, and longing, eagerly longing, to be able to vindicate her own rights. ·Still, whatever ſhe may urge, it will have little weight, if avarice or luxury oppoſe her claim. We are exceedingly ready, it is the turn of the age, to expreſs ourſelves ſorrowfully, when any act of oppreſſion, or unjuſt ſuffering, is related before us; the generous ſentiment flows glibly off our tongues, charity ſeems to dictate every ſympathizing phraſe, and vanity comes cheerfully forward to make her offering. But whom ſhall we find willing to ſacrifice his amuſement or his pleaſure, to obey the call of humanity? Who to relieve the ſufferings of the wretched ſlave, will boldly encounter the oppreſſor's rage, or offer up ſelfiſh intereſt at the altar of mercy? Why, then, hath the active zeal of the benevolent Mr. Granville Sharp, and a few others, in the buſineſs that we now agitate, hitherto made the unfeeling indifference of our age, and nation, but the more conſpicuous?

We muſt not therefore ſtop at gaining over humanity to our ſide, but go on to ſhew, that ſociety is deeply intereſted in advancing the condition of ſlaves, and that it would even be for the benefit of their immediate maſters, that they ſhould be ſubject only to the laws. As the cravings of luxury and extravagance have of late begun to make inroads, even on the ſlave's

partial

partial refpite from toil on the fabbath; we will, in the mean time fhew, till this much-to-be-defired freedom can be brought gradually about, how much the mafter fins, not only againft heaven, but his own immediate intereft, when he forces his flave to toil for him on this facred day. And fo low is their ftate, that we fhall not intirely lofe the purpofe of this undertaking, if we vindicate for them only their legal claim to this indulgence. To make the reader the better acquainted with the fubject of our inquiry, we will premife a fhort account of the prefent importance of the flaves in our fugar colonies. And we hope to leave felfifhnefs, and private intereft, without excufe, for continuing the heavy yoke which now opprelfes them.

S E C T. I.

Their prefent Importance to Society as Slaves.

IN treating of this fubject, the author finds a difficulty in fuppreffing his feelings. How fhall a man, who is firmly convinced that religion, and law, muft go hand in hand, and extend their influence over every individual, in order to fecure the full purpofes of fociety, pafs over, without cenfure, a conduct both in governors and people, which, refpecting our colonies, is wholly regardlefs of thefe important points;

even

even among thofe, who have always been acknowledged as citizens? All civilized ftates,
hitherto, have had an eftablifhed religion. An
eftablifhed religion has a ftrong influence on
every mode that is tolerated, though not eftablifhed. The church of England, particularly,
is confidered by all fober people, as the great
ftay of the conftitution; and it is a fact, that
the enemies of the one always aim their attacks
at the other. But in the places of which I
write, with hardly one exception, neither is law
animated by religion, nor is religion fupported
by law. Even common opinion has no check
to oppofe to the moft fcandalous crimes, nor
does it operate to reftrain the moft indecent
enormities.*

This

* In this picture, I mean not a general charge of depravity,
but of careleffnefs and indolence, that fix neither punifhment
nor difgrace on the greateft irregularities. When it is confidered, that neither religion nor common opinion have any
check in thefe iflands on perfonal behaviour, it is not fo furprizing that many heinous crimes fhould fhew themfelves, as
that they fhould continue to be confined to the fmaller number
in a country, where law attends to nothing but the fecurity of
a man's property.

It is indeed true of the inhabitants, that though fome individuals may, and actually do, commit the moft flagrant offences, not without punifhment only, but even without blufh-
ing, yet they are in general much better than their rulers.
Within thefe five years, the grand jury of a certain colony
ftrove in vain to bring the complicated crime of murder and
inceft to a trial. The whole bench of juftices, and king's
council, without even fuppofing the man innocent, united to
oppofe

This obfervation of the neglect of all appearance of religion in the colonies is truly difcouraging, and leads directly to this juft and mournful conclufion concerning flaves: " That " the government which pays no attention to " the moral and religious conduct of its liege " fubjects, can be expected to do but little for " the improvement of flaves." In thefe we behold a wretched race of mortals, who are confidered as mere machines or inftruments of our profit, of our luxury, of our caprice, without feelings, without rights, without profpects : —Defpifed beings, who have found no friend, helper, or protector ; who have not influence with a legiflature, that from year to year is employed in making acts in favour of horned cattle, and afcertaining the rights of partridges and dogs, to get a ftatute paffed, (I will not fay for their benefit as reafonable creatures, but) for their feelings and utility as mere animals, or inftruments of labour ; who cannot procure an edict to prevent the leaft particle of the unalienable rights of human nature from being wrefted out of their poffeffion, by the ignorance,
prejudice,

---

oppofe the attempt, and protect the culprit, and were able to do it effectually.

Barbadoes is almoft the only colony, where any tolerable degree of decency is preferved, refpecting an eftablifhed religion; and though there be many and grievous defects in its conftitution and government, yet this circumftance gives it confiderable advantages in point of decency and civilization above the others, efpecially the new iflands.

prejudice, cruelty, revenge, and felfifhnefs of untaught, inconfiderate men, their mafters and their overfeers. And this neglect they meet with from a legiflature, whofe chief conftitutional purpofe of affembling, is to difpofe of their conftituents money, and which, from a very natural inquiry, might have known, that while the flaves in our fugar colonies, exceeded not the fortieth part of the inhabitants of the empire, at the breaking out of the late war, they contributed, in that neglected ftate, perhaps nearly a fixth part of its then revenue : a proportion which might be confiderably increafed, if the condition of the miferable wretches themfelves were a little improved.

As this is a bold affertion, it will be necelfary to fhew, on what *data* I proceed*, in the difcuffion of a fubject, in which exactnefs cannot be expected. I had made my calculations

before

* The inhabitants of England and }
   Wales are eftimated at   }   7,500,000
Scotland   1,500,000
Ireland   2,500,000

                              11,500,000

BRITISH ISLES, &c.

North America Freemen 2,600,000
————— Slaves   400,000—3,000,000
Sugar Colonies Freemen   82,000
————— Slaves   418,000— 500,000
       Colonies   3,500,000

   Empire   15,000,000

before America was declared independent, Ireland made a separate state, and Tobago, with all its improvements, given up to France; and it is a subject of too much chagrin, to adapt them now to our new condition.

The sugar colonies produce sugar, rum, coffee, cocoa, cotton, ginger, pimento, indigo, tobacco, aloes, mahogany, sweetmeats, &c. These valued all as casks of raw sugar, each of 1200 lb. at the King's beam, London, may be estimated in moderately productive years, as below. To complete the view, the inhabitants are added.

Islands	Free Inhabitants	Slaves	Staple reduced to casks of Sugar
Barbadoes	20,000	80,000	24,000
Tobago	1,000	8,000	6,000
Grenada and Grenadillas	7,000	30,000	36,000
St. Vincent's	4,000	15,000	10,000
Dominica,	4,000	15,000	10,000
Antigua	6,000	36,000	20,000
Montserrat	2,000	9,000	6,000
Nevis	2,000	10,000	8,000
St. Christopher's	3,000	27,000	20,000
Anquilla, Tortola and its Dependencies	3,000	14,000	10,000
Jamaica & its Dependencies	30,000	174,000	100,000
Total	82,000	418,000	250,000

The sugar baker in Britain pays for sugar, the chief article, from £24 to £30 per cask. Hence the value of the staple is seldom below

£6,000,000

£6,000,000 per annum. The flaves eftimated at £50 each will exceed the fum of 20,000,000. The lands, buildings, and other ftock, may be fet down at twice this fum, or £40,000,000. We have then the Weft-Indian ftock, exceeding £60,000,000 and giving a yearly produce of 6,000,000. About £1,000,000 of this laft comes into the exchequer, for duties on fugar, rum, &c. And there cannot be lefs than £800,000 raifed on the trade of the iflands, and on the planters, who refide, and fpend their fortunes in England. The freight, agency, light-houfe money, ftorage, infurance, and other incidental charges, are a full million more of gain to Britain. And as the whole is put in motion, and draws its worth from the labour of flaves, it clearly proves their prefent importance, and their claim to national attention.

Indeed, the whole balance of their annual produce may be fuppofed as remaining with Britain. For there is not referved in the colonies, a part fufficient to make the neceffary improvements, in many cafes, not even to keep up the ftock. And even what is fpent in the iflands, is laid out in the purchafe of Britifh or American commodities; but much the largeft fhare is kept in Britain, to be fpent, or to pay the intereft of five or fix millions of money due there. In fhort, they may be confidered as manufactories eftablifhed in convenient diftant places, that

draw

draw all their utenfils from, and fend all their produce to, the mother country.

I have fuppofed the medium produce to be £6,000,000, as the prime coft in Britain; but after paffing through the hands of the manufacturer, it muft coft the confumer full £8,000,000.

S E C T. II.

Their prefent importance to Society would be increafed by Freedom.

FROM this view of the importance of our flaves, in their prefent ftate, (for they alone ftamp a value on Weft-Indian property) it will clearly follow, that to improve and advance their condition in focial, to enccurage and inftruct them in moral life, would be as politically profitable, as it is religious and humane. Were their condition advanced, they would become more worthy, more valuable fubjects. They would produce much more by their labour, and agreeably to that great purpofe of modern police, financeering, by the confumption of more manufactures, they would increafe the public revenue.*

Inftead

---

* A French author fneers at Boyle, for propofing to propagate Chriftianity among favages, with a view to make them

F   wear

· Inftead of confining their demands, as at prefent, to a few coarfe woollens and Ofnaburgs,
to a little grain, a few herrings, and falt-fifh,
they would open a new traffic in every branch
of trade, and while they improved our commerce, they would add to the ftrength and fecurity of the colonies. The few, who by accident, or indulgence, have been advanced in focial life, make even now a confiderable addition
to the internal confumption of the white inhabitants. And how much to be preferred, a
numerous free peafantry is to a few over-grown
families, and their herds of naked, half ftarved
flaves, is too evident to need explanation.

There are about 30,000 inhabitants in St.
Chriftopher's, of which not more than one in
ten is free. They are in dread of infurrections
in time of peace, and in time of war are expofed to every fort of depredation; every pitiful
privateer, while hovering around, alarming the
coaft, and endangering their fafety. For at
thefe times the flaves, far from adding to their
                                            ftrength,

---

wear clothes, and thereby increafe the demand for Englifh
manufactures. Perhaps he aimed to catch men, by the bait
of intereft, who were dead to fentiments of religion and humanity. Still the obfervation fhews, how much a progrefs in
religion draws after it focial advantages, and civilization, of
which the Moravian miffions in Greenland are a moft convincing proof.

ftrength, weaken and diminifh it. But if all the inhabitants were free, and had property and families to fight for, what fhould they have to fear, who could draw out full 8000 hardy men, habituated to the climate, and, within five hours, have them ranged in order againft any enemy that might affail them.

That fugar may be made by white labourers, appeared in the firft fettlement of our iflands, efpecially Barbadoes. In the moft flourifhing ftate of that Ifland, the fugar-cane was chiefly cultivated by white fervants. It has fenfibly and gradually decayed in trade and importance, fince the majority of its inhabitants has been changed from free-men to flaves. The ftock of the planter has indeed been increafed with the number, and the price of his flaves; but his neat produce has not kept pace with it. Even after this ifland had been fome time on the decline, one plantation *(the Bell)* fitted out a company of foldiers for the expedition formed in 1691, under Codrington, againft Guadaloupe. If there be now on the fame fpot, four white men, including the proprietor, able to bear arms, it is a great proportion. From this we may judge, how much the ifland has fince loft in trade and fecurity, even after allowing largely in the calculation. Yet it continues

F 2   to

to fupport a greater proportion of free-men than
our other iflands. *

To this inftance of making fugar by freemen,
we may add the example of Cochin China. It
fupplies the populous empire of China with fugar, made by free-men. The quantity exported is eftimated at 800,000,000 pound, or a-
bout 500,000 of cafks, which greatly exceeds
the quantity of fugar made in the ifles, and
continent of America, by African flaves. And
this quantity may be fuppofed capable of being
greatly increafed, if the manufacture was carried on in the fame accurate manner as in the
European colonies. For, according to Le
Poivre, the cane juice is only boiled into fyrup
at the place of growth, and in that flate is
carried to the feveral towns, to be fold to the
fugar baker, who boils, refines, and candies it.
After this tedious procefs, brown fugar is fold
at 3s. 4d. per hundred pound, white fugar
6s. 8d. and candied fugar at 8s. In our iflands
brown fugar is worth by the 100 pound, from
20s. to 36s. fterling, and yet many of our
proprietors cannot pay their intereft-money, and
fupport their flock, without fuppofing any fhare
of

* About the time of the reftoration, the ifland of St. Chriftopher's contained about 10,000 French and Englifh, capable of
bearing arms. About 1650, Nevis could arm above 5000.
The whole prefent militia of both iflands exceeds not 1000,
Such a deftroyer is flavery of population.

of the produce to be allotted as the returns of their own capital.

S E C T. III.

Their Masters would be profited by their advancement.

I T might be difficult for government to form a plan, that should at once extend full liberty to, and thereby bestow due rank on our slaves, without immediately indangering the property of their masters, and of the trading part of the nation connected with them in busi-ness and interest. And it must be acknow-ledged, that such at present is the ignorant, helpless condition of far the greater part of the slaves, that full liberty would be no blessing to them. They need a master to provide and care for them. The plan, proposed to advance and instruct them, must be gentle, slow in its pro-gress, keeping pace with the opening of their minds, and looking forward for its completion to a distant period.

The slaves, in that little spot, St. Christo-pher's, moderately appraised, would exceed £1,300,000, and as they are part of a stock of £4,000,000, and give effect and life to

that

that flock, the fruits of their labours being in moft years worth to the confumers, £ 700,000, it is evident that an immenfe change or rather annihilation of property would be occafioned, if this fcheme took at once effect in the colonies; nor would it be poffible to find the mafters an equivalent.

While I acknowledge this in favour of the mafter, as things are now fituated, I am firmly of opinion, that a fugar plantation might be cultivated to more advantage, and at much lefs expence, by labourers who were free-men, than by flaves. Men who, like flaves, are ill treated, ill clothed, and worfe fed, who labour not with any view to their own profit, but for that of a mafter, whom for his barbarity they perhaps abhor, have not ftrength, nor fpirits, nor hope to carry them through their tafk. A free-man, labouring for himfelf, in the earning of his wages, whofe food is portioned out by himfelf, not by an unfeeling boy overfeer; who feels his own vigour, who looks forward to the conveniences of life as connected with his induftry, will furely exert more ftrength, will fhew more alacrity, than a ftarved, depreffed, difpirited wretch, who drawls out his tafk with the whip over him.

It is a common day's labour, where the work is carefully performed, for thirty grown flaves

to

to dig with hoes, in a loofe gravelly foil, an
acre of ground, into holes of five feet by four,
from about feven to twelve inches deep, leaving
fpaces between the rows equal at leaft to half
the holes, untouched, to receive the mould.
The fhare of fuch a piece of work to one flave,
will be a fpot of nearly fifty by thirty feet,
including the untouched fpaces. A tafk this,
that might be more than doubled, by a labourer
of ordinary ftrength, having fpirits and inclination to the work.

In St. Chriftopher's, 16,000 flaves, all capable
of fome labour, are employed in the cultivation
of about 11,000 acres; for the whole cane-
land of the ifland is about 22,000 acres, and each
field gives a crop once in two years. This is
in the proportion of three flaves to the annual
culture of two acres; a rate that would be
unneceffary among free-men, and which the
Britifh prices for Weft Indian produce could
alone fupport. It may be remarked, that this
labour has no winter ceffation.

The common appraifement of prime field
flaves, before the American war, was £60
fterling each; the annual rent of a flave was
from £6 to £8. The renter enfured them, if
valued, at five per cent. or £3 more. A plantation flave cofts the employer then, without
reckoning food, clothes, phyfic, or taxes, full
£10

£10 per annum, or one fixth part of his appraifed
value. A number of flaves, capable of producing on a. plantation, well furnifhed with live
ftock and neceffary buildings, 100 cafks of fugar,
annually at a medium, making but a moderate
allowance for their deaths in feafoning, if bought
from the flave-merchant, will amount on value,
to £6000. In the new iflands, before fuch a
number could be relied on, they have in every
cafe coft much more; in one, within the author's
knowledge, above the double of this fum. The
quantity of fugar here fuppofed, and the rum
arifing from it, in moft fituations will not keep
the plantation in neceffary ftores, and pay the
current expences, and fupply a fund to anfwer
fuch accidents as hurricanes, blafts, fire, morta-
lity, and unfavourable feafons, and alfo give
£1200 to the proprietor, as the produce of
his lands, buildings, flaves, and other ftock.

If his flaves be confidered as rented from
another man, and he infures them to the owner,
£1000 of this £1200 is immediately to be
ftruck off, as the value of the flaves labour.
There remains to the proprietor £200, as the
return of his lands, buildings, and cattle. In fuch
a plantation the buildings often have coft £3000
fterling, fometimes more; the cattle, horfes,
and mules muft be worth from £600 to £1000.
Perhaps the proprietor has paid from £10,000
to £12,000 for the lands, The reader
may

may be affured this is no ideal calculation, but in the ifland of St. Chriftopher, though our moft produ&ive fugar colony in proportion to its fize, has frequently come within the author's obfervation. And is labour fo injudicioufly laid out in any other part of the world ? Can any reafons be given, why a fugar planter fhould prefer the employing of flaves to that of freemen, feeing with a large diminution of returns, he may have a much larger clear income than at prefent. An argument, that when duly weighed, renders our expe&ations of the extenfion of liberty, though diftant, not extravagant.

But we will confider the policy of employing flaves purchafed with money, in another point of view. In a free country, a peafant in general executes twice the work of a flave in the fugar colonies; we might go farther, but this is fufficient for our purpofe. On the other hand the peafant's food is more found, more plentiful, his clothes more expenfive than thofe of a flave; but not in proportion to the difference in value of their labour, perhaps not exceeding greatly the infurance, and other incidental charges of flavery. In general, this food and raiment are all that the peafant, as well as the flave, reaps from his labour, few of them raifing themfelves by their induftry to a fuperior ftation ; and when they do this, it is effe&ed by fuperior induftry, or keennefs, and greater parfimony, parſimony, rather than by extraordinary wages. The whole then of a peaſant's labour (that proportion excepted, which the ſlave in a certain degree alſo claims from his toil) becomes the profit and property of his employer, as fully and truly as if he were a ſlave; with this difference in favour of the firſt, that the obligation, or tie between him and his maſter, ends with the day's, or year's labour, and draws no diſagreeable or expenſive conſequences after it, to either of the parties.

Now from the ſuperior progreſs of population in free countries, compared with that of thoſe wherein ſlavery prevails, when a peaſant dies, his place is immediately ſupplied in the courſe of generation; the employer ſuffers no damage, or loſs of time; and while labour and improvement go equally on, even the public, to which every perſon in a free ſtate may be ſaid to belong, is not ſenſible of the event. In ſhort, in a free ſtate, the death of an individual is like a ſtone caſt into the water, it makes a ſudden ſeparation of the parts, but the water cloſes on it, and ſettles into a ſmooth ſurface, as if no accident had preceded. But to his maſter, the death of a ſlave is a ſenſible ſevere loſs, which he muſt immediately repair, at an heavy expence, that, after being incurred, will not make him the ſame profitable returns, as the labour of a peaſant for which he pays (and that not till
after

after the execution of the work) only fuch a value as he ought to expend in the maintenance of his flaves. The eftimation of ufeful flaves, without taking luft, caprice, or favour into account, is according to their trades and accomplifhments, from £ 50 to £ 300 fterling. Hence the death of a valuable flave becomes a moft ferious matter to the mafter, while a peafant, or tradefman, will do him fuperior fervice, without original expence, or daily rifk to him, or to the public.

This is a view of the fubjeƐt, and a manner of reafoning in it, which cannot, I apprehend, be controverted, and plainly proves, that could we contrive a method of once getting over the firft fhock, which fuch a change would occafion, and fet down free-men and women (who in the common progrefs of population, might fupport or increafe their original number, in our colonies) in the room of flaves, we fhould leffen the nominal value of the neceffary ftock, contraƐt the expences of individuals, and much more than double their prefent profit. Here, then, we have an argument againft flavery, which applies equally to the intereft of the mafter, and the advantage of the public, and ought to gain a fair hearing for every plan, that propofes to leffen the numbers, and advance the condition of flaves. And were we not afraid of ftartling the imaginations of people, by the extraordinary affertion,

affertion, we would not hefitate to affirm, that
were the minds of the negroes once opened, and
properly prepared; and were they in general
confined to the cultivation of Weft-Indian produce, and the trades connected with it; and did
government introduce from time to time, till
things became fettled on the new bafis, at the
expence of the colony, the neceffary recruits;
the general manumiffion of flaves would be
attended with no immediate lofs to the planters;
and, by taking away the neceffity of fupplying
themfelves with recruits at their own expence,
would be an important faving to them.   Indeed,
after one generation, recruits would not be
wanted; freedom would *increafe* fafter than
death *lffened* their numbers. *

A ftate

---

* The reader will be pleafed with the following fenfible
remarks of a gentleman of Barbadoes, on his perufing this fec-
tion in manufcript.

Barbadoes, of all the Weft-Indian iflands, can the leaft afford the immenfe expenfe of an annual fupply of flaves. As
the white inhabitants are numerous, flavery might be abolifhed
in a few years, without an individual fuffering by it. The
majority of the inhabitants are indigent. There are numbers
of flaves, who, having been taught trades, are become highly
valuable, of whom, one, two, or a few, are frequently the only
fupport of whole white families, who live in indolent poverty
on the returns of their labour, and by their death find themfelves reduced to the utmoft diftrefs, and incapable of doing
any thing for themfelves. If this fort of precarious property
were not univerfally relied on, fo as to have a general ill effect
on the manners of the people, they would of neceffity be forced
to be more induftrious in themfelves, and more œconomical in
their

. A ftate of abfolute freedom is indeed a revolution that we may rather wifh for, than expect
for fome time to fee, though doubtlefs it is
within the plan of Providence, and of man's
progreffive advancement in fociety. It fuppofes
a regard for religion, a looking beyond immediate
profit, and a.foundnefs of policy, foreign to the
eftimation, and opinion of the prefent age. To
make the plan effectual, it fhould prevail in
every

their expences. If flavery were checked, the poor white people, who, at prefent, (from the circumftance of their living
meanly idle on the labours of others,) are perhaps the moft
lifelefs, inactive fet of mortals, on the whole earth, would be
obliged to exert themfelves in the cultivation of their own, and
others lands, and foon would perceive their conftitutions and circumftances equally improved   The great land-holders would
find their expences and their profits go hand in hand; for they
would pay only for productive labour.   The moft induftrious
labourers would command the beft employment, and the moft
punctual pay would conftantly have the preference.   Thus
punctuality and application would encourage each other, renew the face of the colony, and put the whip and chain to
fhame.   It would be a great ftep towards this defirable purpofe, if the introduction of flaves into the colony was prohibit-
ed by ftatute, and all acts that lay fines upon thofe mafters
who free their flaves, were repealed.   Every method fhould
be ufed, that would induce the people to refpect the inftitutions
of religion, and wean them from that carelefnefs refpecting
them, which is fo prevalent, and has fuch baneful effects on their
manners.   The flaves in Barbadoes are perhaps more ripe for
thefe privileges than thofe of our other colonies; becaufe the
proportion of Creoles, or natives, is greater among them; they
are more converfant with the free people, and are lefs pinned
down than in other iflands to digging the ground.   It is
certain, they have in their prefent ftate been at different times
trufted with arms; corps of them have been formed, and on all
occafions have difcovered an alacrity that promifed every poffible exertion.

every European fettlement ; an event fo little to be expected from the manners which now prevail, that a man would not venture the imputation of fuch extravagance, as the bare fuggeftion of it would be deemed. For could fo many oppofing interefts be reconciled ; and fhould a partial innovation take place, that prefent bugbear of European policy, the balance of trade, would be fuppofed to be in danger.

But were flaves inftructed in the fimple pre-cepts of religion ; were they taught to diftinguifh right from wrong ; did the law fecure to them a more plentiful fubfiftence, more humane ufage ; were they permitted to acquire and enjoy pro-perty ; were the rights of a family made facred ; could they look forward to freedom, as the reward of merit, or the purchafe of induftry ; in fhort, were they confidered as having fome rights, fome claims, as intitled to fome unalienable, fome of the referved rights of humane nature ; their condition would in confequence be ad-vanced, they would become more ufeful, more profitable fubjects, and might even be trufted with arms, in defence of the colony in which they have an intereft. Indeed it is not their want of arms, but their good fenfe and modera-tion, in moft colonies, that are a prefent fecurity to the inhabitants.   I. forbear to fay more on fo dangerous a topic.*

S E C T.

* It is worthy of obfervation, that though the artificers in the King's dock yards had, from their firft eftablifhment, been engaged,

S E C T. IV.

Their Mafters would be profited by allowing their Slaves the privilege of a weekly Sabbath.

WE have proved, that the gradual extenfion of freedom would have the beft effects refpecting both

engaged, and liberally paid, by the day, yet within thefe twelve years, it has been found moft expedient to employ and pay them by the piece, or job ; the men earning more, and the public getting more work, and that cheaper done, than in the former method, when they juft drawled out the prefcribed number of hours, and like Cyrus's well-trained foldier, would fufpend the up-lifted axe, at the firft ftroke of the bell that called them off from their work. Good farmers alfo employ labourers, wherever they can, by the piece, and induftrious men prefer it, as being mutually moft profitable. In Kent where there is the greateft variety of agriculture, almoft every kind of work is paid for by the piece or job.

If moderate fkilful planters would fet down, and reduce into a table, the feveral rates of negro-labour, by the day, and a ftatute were enacted, that fhould give the flave, who had per-formed this tafk, the reft of his time to himfelf, or intitle him to wages for what he fhould do more than this; and if all flaves were valued, and permitted by this their extra work gradually to buy out themfelves, or their time ; and if it were only provided, that after they became free, they fhould con-tinue to be employed about the bufinefs of a plantation; in this fituation, planters might have the original coft of their flaves repaid them, and would ftill have the fame people to do their work better than at prefent, for food and raiment; only fewer in number would anfwer their purpofe, and their intereft would not be affected by any accident that befel them. The labourers, on the other hand, when their jobs were finifhed, would

both the master and the community. But it
will require new regulations, and the consent of
government and people, to establish the plan.
What follows here has already the sanction of
law, and is now the practice, in proportion
to the discretion and fellow-feeling of the
master. The infringement on that rest of the
sabbath, which we wish to vindicate for the
slave, is an indecent breach, both of religion
and law, while it counteracts, in no small degree, its own mean purpose of accumulation.
But such is the progressive nature of the cravings
of luxury and avarice, that if the custom once
gets a footing, reason in vain will solicit an
hearing ; and religion has lost her influence, and
law her authority, should they attempt to
interpose.

would be their own masters, and be able to enjoy themselves, and their families. They would feel an ambition to
become worthy members of society, and to partake, with their
former masters, now become their patrons and benefactors,
in the institutions of a religion, that considered them all as
equally the children of the same benevolent Father. One immediate consequence of the relaxation of slavery, would be the
introduction of ploughs, which have always answered where-
ever they have been tried, and are only thrown aside, because
it is easier for a manager to order out a slave with his hoe in his
hand, than to yoke horses or cattle in a plough. It is indeed
a maxim, in carrying on all labour, never to do that by a man,
that you can execute by a brute ; nor to do that by an animal,
that you can make a mechanical instrument perform. Thus
all hand-hoe ploughing, except in particular cases, would be
cut off, and all cattle mills for grinding canes would be ex-
changed for water or wind mills. This method of working
out freedom by labour is said to be established by a law in the
Spanish colonies, for the encouragement of their slaves.

interpofe. Our only hope remains in being able to pre-occupy the judgment. As this refers to a particular event in one of our colonies, which is too likely to take place in others, the arguments are prefented to the public in their original drefs; and thofe, who are beft acquainted with the treatment that flaves ufually meet with, will be leaft apt to imagine that the author has been too full, or too warm on the fubject.

An ADDRESS *to the* INHABITANTS *of* ST. CHRISTOPHER's, *Anno,* 1775, *fhewing the Claim of Dependents to the Privilege of the Sabbath.*

SIRS,

Within thefe laft ten months, a cuftom has been introduced among you, of employing flaves in carrying on the ordinary plantation work on Sunday, of ploughing the ground, planting, weeding, and grinding the cane, boiling the fugar, and diftilling the rum. It began on a particular plantation, and has found its way to each extremity of the ifland. It is true, it is not yet become general, and many planters firmly exprefs their diflike of a practice, which, in itfelf impolitic and injudicious, bids fair, if encouraged, to banifh humanity, and annihilate a religion that barely ftruggles for exiftence in our land. But bad examples are contagious; and feeming intereft in fome and emulation in others

will

will go on, as they already have begun, to draw numbers into a cuſtom that flatters induſtry, and feeds the hopes of extravagance and avarice.

No account of this ſpreading violation of our laws and religion having yet been taken by the magiſtracy, the treſpaſſers are induced to believe that law cannot interpoſe to check it : a miſtake which it is neceſſary to correct in men, who think nothing a crime but a deed for which law ordains a puniſhment. As it fell to my lot to take the firſt notice of this unhallowed practice, I have been obliged to pay an atten-tion to the ſubject ; and hence I am enabled to aſſure theſe treſpaſſers, who wrap themſelves up in their impunity, that when the caſe is brought before a court, they will not find a lawyer, however profligate his private character may be, who will riſk his profeſſional reputation by undertaking the defence of ſo notorious a breach of human and divine laws : and could they find ſuch a man, no judge or bench of magiſtrates could allow him to plead againſt the laws and religion of his country. Their defence muſt be confined to a ſimple denial of the fact.

If we view the matter in a religious light, the ſabbath is appointed by God for ſuch pious, humane, and even wordly-wiſe purpoſes, as to lead us to conclude, that nothing will more rea-dily draw down judgments on, nor ſooner exe-cute

cute the ruin of, a finful community, than a contempt of this benevolent inftitution. Sabbath-breaking makes a conftant capital figure among the crimes that kindled God's wrath againft the Jews. Farther, from God's ftrict injunction to them, from whom we derive this inftitution, to punifh, even to deftruction, any family or city that they fhould find guilty of idolatry among them, which was an offence fimply againft his authority; we may conclude, that if a community fuffers an infult on this law of the fabbath, which has both his authority and general benevolence in view, to pafs unpunifhed, it will, by fuch its neglect, fubject to his wrath not only individuals that are actually guilty of the crime, but the magiftracy and people at large, who are thus carelefs of vindicating his honour and the claims of humanity. I will leave it to yourfelves, after what you have lately fuffered in your fins, to determine what need you have to give the Governor of the world this new provocation againft you. Woe be to that community which forces the Deity to refume the vindication of his laws from the hands of the ordinary magiftrate. Undiftinguifhing ruin will involve the lukewarm profeffor and hardy trefpaffer together. May Providence, by your reformation, avert the evil which every thinking man dreads on your account. To contribute to this end, and fet fuch right as

have

have been unwittingly drawn into the practice, who yet have minds open to conviction, we submit to them the following confiderations :

The good man, on the fabbath, interrupts his ufual employments, not only to have leifure to review his conduct, to improve his mind for futurity, to reflect on, and blefs God for his mercies, but alfo for the fake of his dependents : they are indulged with a refpite from labour, and a weekly feftival, which make fervitude tolerable.   This compaffion is followed by its proper reward.   Continual toil would wear out the conftitutions of fervants long before their natural period of decay ; but, during this day of reft, they renew their ftrength, and the hopes of its weekly return make them chearfully undergo their common labour.   The ufeful ox repays the indulgence in patient enduring.

Indeed, this day of reft, which God commands us to allow all whom he hath fubmitted to our rule, is an acknowledgment, that he . obligeth us to pay for the dominion he hath granted us over the lower world.   And, therefore, though the promulgation and extent of this precept reft on the pofitive command of God expreffed in fcripture, yet is the foundation moral : it is laid deep in the principles of humanity, grows up with obedience to our Creator, and flourifheth with equity and benevolence to

our

our fellow-creatures. It is a mark of holding our power from God, a right referved to himfelf, to fhew his care of even the meaneft of his creatures. And it teacheth us, in a manner plain for him that runneth to read it, that we had not our prefent rank in the creation beftowed on us, to be the unfeeling tyrants, but the merciful protectors, of the inferior world.

But as a contrary practice is now introduced here, with a parade, indeed, of fuperior induftry, but a fovereign contempt of decency, common opinion, religion, and law ; we muft difcufs this point of indulgence to dependents, and fhew, (befides contradicting the motives above, which I hope have yet fome influence among mankind) that he, who falls into fo inconfiderate a practice, fins againft prudence, and counteracts that aim after opulence, which can be the only pretence for fo extraordinary, fo alarming a conduct. In doing this, we need not enter into any nice phyfical difquifition concerning the animal powers of the labouring part of the creation, nor into any train of reafoning, to fhew the neceffity of a frequent fucceffion of reft to labour to preferve the animal machine from wearing out before the period fet by nature : we will appeal to your own experience, whether thofe men reap not the moft lafting advantages from the labour of their oxen, their horfes, and that ftill more ufeful, though neglected animal,

mal, called a negroe flave, who confult their
feveral feelings, and give the fignal to ceafe from
toil, before the languid effort of wearinefs folicits refpite. Are they the moft fuccefsful in
the field of induftry, or do they moft enjoy the
evening of life, who conftantly put forth all
their ftrength, who rife early, and late take
reft; or they, who fo temper labour and reft,
that each defires the return of the other. Look
around among your neighbours, whofe flaves,
whofe cattle, are the moft healthy, or exert the
greateft vigour; who fuffers leaft by their mor-
tality; who reaps moft from their labour? Is it
not he who encourages, favours, fpares them,
who properly nourifhes them, and never en-
croaches on the hour of food or reft? Or can
any temporary acquifition, wrung from unfea-
fonable labour, compenfate for an hofpital filled
with wretches dead or dying, for a crew of
haggard, difeafed fpeƐtres, whofe ruined conftitutions, and famifhed looks, reproach the avarice
of the hard-hearted mafter.

Is it faid, in return, that the mafter buys this
extraordinary labour, on Sunday, with an extraordinary price. Let me afk him, who gives
this reafon, would he pufh a generous horfe,
till the noble animal himfelf gave out? And is
he to care lefs for a creature of his own kind,
becaufe anxious to recommend himfelf to his favour by a ftrained exertion of his ftrength? The
mafter,

mafter, by the very tenure of his authority is obliged to confult the conftitution of thofe who labour for him, that he may reftrain their efforts within their ability, and keep their fervice to him within the limits of their own perfonal happinefs. If, as fome pretend, it be meant to increafe the allowance of food, by this new cuftom of Sunday's wages, let them tell why, till now, they have provided fo fcantily for their flaves, as to make this addition neceffary; or let them give a good reafon why a wretch who drudges the fix days for another man's luxury, fhould not eat plentifully, and have the feventh alfo for a day of reft.

If the planter fays he only bribes other mens flaves into his Sunday's fervice, let him go to his neighbour, and afk him for the ufe of his cattle during the hours allotted for food and reft, and report his anfwer; or let him attempt to take them away, and work them clandeftinely, and fee whether they will not be reclaimed. And fhall a confiderate mafter, who works his flaves to their full ability; and who, it fhould be prefumed, feeds them properly, fuffer them to wear their ftrength out in another man's fervice for a little paultry hire, that ought not to be neceffary for them? Or, if he did, could he expect them to exert themfelves with vigour for him in the week, when their ftrength has been worn
down

down in his neighbour's fervice on Sunday, and they have not had time to recruit it? God who beft knows the conftitution of his creatures, and formed them exprefsly for labour, hath allotted for reft not only the nightly fucceffion of dark-nefs and weekly return of the fabbath, but has divided every fingle day into fhort intervals of labour and reft, by making a frequent repetition of food neceffary for recruiting and refrefhing the body. And fhall we pretend to be wifer than he is, or to know better what the animal conftitution is capable of performing?

One reafon is given for this cuftom, which puts the obfervation of Sunday as a day of reft, on plantations, wholly in the overfeers power: if a flave behaves to the fatisfaction of the overfeer throughout the week, he is to be indulged with Sunday, if not he fhall work there on his mafter's field. And this humane reafon is added, that the common punifhment of withholding their ufual allowance of food is injudicious, and therefore working on Sunday is fubftituted for it. I am ready to give up the propriety of ftarving men as a mode of punifh-ment. But is not the obliging them to work on Sundays alfo to ftarve them; feeing, in the prefent pinched method of feeding them, every flave is forced to eke out his portion with his private Sundays labour? And doth not this extraordinary labour on Sunday act as a farther leffening leſſening of their allowance, by wearing out their ſtrength in toiling on the day in which they ſhould have had leiſure to recruit it after the week's labour, while the means of acquiring food by private labour to repair this extraordinary waſte are withheld from them.

But we give Sunday, as a day of reſt to our ſlaves, in obedience to the command of our common Father. And nothing but a duty, ſuperior in its conſequences, and immediate in its call, or an unforeſeen opportunity of doing an act of benevolence can ſet it aſide. Now as a duty owing immediately to God, it cannot be affected by any pretended intereſt of our own, or demerit on our ſervants part. Are God's laws to be ſo little eſteemed of, that every unthinking boy, ſet over a few helpleſs wretches, with a whip in his hand, may annul them at pleaſure? Shall he, to puniſh a trifling offence againſt the plantation diſcipline, too frequently exiſting only in his own miſapprehenſion or neglect, be allowed to make havock of the laws of religion and his own duty to God? Unhappy age into which we are fallen, when, leaving the plain road of obedience, we ſet up to reform the laws and religion, not of our country only, but of our God!

It is ſuggeſted further, that in crop time, in particular quarters, the ripe canes are ſo apt

G   to

to become tainted, that it is a work of neceſſity to grind them off on Sunday. To this we
anſwer, " The God of ſeaſons enjoined the
obſervation of the ſabbath, and his laws are
ultimately for the benefit of the obedient."
The circumſtance here pleaded may be intended for an exerciſe of our truſt in his Providence, but can never come under the deſcrip-
tion of thoſe works of neceſſity or mercy, that
are not only proper, but commendable on Sunday. Sagacity may foreſee, prudence may provide for ſuch accidents ; method and good uſage
may, and where uſed, actually *do*, increaſe the
tale of labour, on common days, far beyond
what is forced out on this day appointed for
reſt. And were not this, which yet may be,
in every caſe, true, yet God's veracity and
providence are engaged that his ſervants ſhould
not ultimately ſuffer by their obedience. But,
as we have remarked, and ſhall further prove,
the truth is, this continued toil over-acts the
purpoſe of induſtry, without ſuppoſing God,
in his Providence, to puniſh the inſult done to
his laws and religion.

One reaſon is given for this practice, that
carries a face of concern for religion, but is
ſufficiently abſurd, and ſelfiſh in the application. " Slaves cannot keep the ſabbath as
Chriſtians ; and if not employed for their maſters, will labour for themſelves." Now the
trifling

trifling Sundays works, in their own grounds, which an injudicious cuftom has permitted, and their fcanty allowance of food has made neceffary, is done in fuch manner and circum-ftances, as makes it more an amufement than a labour; nor can it be compared with toiling in their mafter's field under the whip of an overfeer. But I can recollect a particular plan-tation, where the manager, fome years ago, with a good intention, made the flaves exert themfelves on Sundays, as much in their own ground, as in their mafter's fields, throughout the week; and the confequence was, that from this inceffant fatigue, the plantation re-quired a yearly fupply of flaves, above a tenth part of the whole number maintained. Since they have been left to their own inclinations on Sundays, they have been moft remarkably healthy; nor, I believe, had or needed a re-cruit thefe laft fixteen years. The plantation is particularly well fupplied with provifions; and the flaves have been treated with peculiar humanity and method.

But if flaves do not hallow the fabbath in a rational manner, cannot their mafters and overfeers, by their own behaviour, fanctify it. And, furely to overlook what you cannot pre-vent in another, differs widely from the com-manding of him to commit a crime, of which you mean to reap the advantage. That flaves

cannot

cannot rationally keep the fabbath is matter of ferious concern. I pray God we may not all be made accountable for it. Still allow this argument what weight you pleafe ; God is the God of the bodies as well as of the fouls of his creatures, and he wills and attends equally to the welfare of both ; and the fabbath is intended to refrefh the one, and improve the other. Oxen and horfes cannot keep a Chriftian fabbath ; yet, their Creator refpects their eafe, and, among other purpofes, appointeth the fabbath exprefsly to favour it. And, furely, God doth not lefs regard the bodily fenfations of human wretches, becaufe in his Providence, for hidden yet certainly wife purpofes, he hath hitherto fuffered them to be immediately fubjected to the caprice, the avarice, the cruelty of their fellows, though endued with keener feelings than the brutes, and greater fenfibility of their claims. Farther, God accepts favourably what fervice and thanks his creatures are able to pay him ; and the fimple rude way in which negroes, in their Sunday's amufements, exprefs their fatisfaction in his difpenfations, will not be rejected, but be received with approbation and condefcenfion to their weaknefs.

When we have made every allowance that charity or confideration can fuggeft, no man acquainted with the ufual progrefs of human affairs, and the conftant tendency of cuftom,

but

but muft fee, in this unhallowed, hired, Sunday's labour, the haftening abolition of refpect to that day, and of extraordinary hire for working on it. Poverty is craving; avarice infatiable; luxury boundlefs. And were Sunday once melted down into the week, men would try what more could be cut off from the darknefs, and folitude, and reft of night.

But without taking into account the inhumanity, the immorality, the imprudence, the irreligion of the practice; what impudence, refpecting fociety, doth it imply, when thus a private man fets his felfifh opinion up againft the laws of his country, and dares to infult them publickly, by acting in direct oppofition to an exprefs ftatute? How pregnant in ill confequences muft the example be, in a community where cuftom has reduced almoft the whole of an eftablifhed religion to bodily reft on the fabbath? Piety, foon, will not have a fingle thread of communication by which to lay hold on our practice. How neceffary, therefore, to fix a mark on fuch profane conduct, before cuftom has ftamped a fafhion on it, and fanctified it? And often, for what is humanity, religion and law thus wounded? To anfwer the demands of extravagance, to fill the bags of avarice, to fupply the funds of luxury. Slavery, in its mildeft fhape, has

fomething

fomething dangerous and threatning to virtue; but when the very marrow and blood of our fellow creatures are exhaufted in the cruel fer- vice of avarice or fenfuality, the equal Father of all muft call in fome dreadful vengeance to punifh the abufe.

I mean not fo much to reflect on indivi- duals, who may already be guilty of this unfeel- ing, imprudent practice, as to exalt to its proper motives of religion, benevolence, and obedience to your country's laws, that abhor- rence which hath been entertained againft an action that is an outrage to common fenfe, and common opinion; and which, we are taught in fcripture, never fails to draw down God's wrath on the people who permit it to be done with impunity among them. It is an offence, which, if not checked in its progrefs, may renew thofe judgments that for our fins were lately poured out on us; under which we now, and long muft continue to fmart; without provoking farther God's vengeance, or obliging him to fend new or extraordinary punifhments to chaftize or reclaim us *. Could I keep you from the contagion of example, I fhould rejoice. Whoever has thus finned

* Since this period this colony has been greatly reduced by fire, floods, war, capture by the enemy, and fuch unfavour- able feafons, as had hardly happened before in the memory of man.

againft

againſt God, and his country, ſhall have my prayers, that he may be inſpired with a right way of thinking. Of this be aſſured, that ſuch an extraordinary mode of induſtry is not the path in which God's bleſſings are to be met with. And they who uſe it have reaſon to fear, left a diſtreſsful turn in their affairs make this day of liberty and reſt, which they want to cut off from ſociety, the only day in which they dare to enjoy their freedom. †

But if God did not, as certainly he doth, mix therewith a ſecret canker, to eat up the ſubſtance of the offender, yet the unfeeling, hurrying mode of thus working ſlaves, would, by waſting their ſtrength and health, be of itſelf ſufficient puniſhment. And, ſuppoſing the obſervation of the ſabbath to depend wholly for its ſanction on revelation, and the breach of it to be followed by no natural loſs, which is far from the truth; yet, if you be diligent and obedient to the law, for God's ſake, he can, in his Providence, and will, in a thouſand ways, make up any imaginary ſacrifice of time and profit to a truſt in his word, and will proceed in an inconceivable manner to bleſs and proſper you.

† It is certain, that he who began this cuſtom within twelve months durſt not on any other day ſhew his face for fear of his creditors.

I ſhall

I fhall conclude with an obfervation drawn from mechanics. Though a man of ordinary ftrength can raife, at a fingle effort, a much greater weight, yet the moft advantageous exertion of it is within thirty pounds weight; and he, who works diligently eight hours a day, will do more work in a week, than he who drawls out in languid exertions fourteen hours.

CHAP.

C H A P. III.

The Advancement of Slaves must accompany their religious Instruction.

I S H A L L confider the advantage of pro-moting flaves in focial life, as proved beyond a poffibility of contradiction ; but, as my parti-cular aim is to get religion extended to them, I muft fhew that there is a connection between focial privileges and religious inftruction ; and that the making of a progrefs in either requires them to go hand in hand, and influence each other. That men were intended both for fociety and religion, and that thefe two were meant to fupport each other, is a conclufion to be drawn from every circumftance that refpects our pow-ers and conftitution. The helplefs ftate of in-fancy, the variety and inequality of our faculties, all attach us to a particular community, fit us for our various ftations in it, and give it an in-diffoluble claim to our fervice and affiftance. And religion brings confcience in to the aid of focial regulations, and fits the man for acting his part in his proper ftation.

Religion has a two-fold purpofe : man's ul-timate fate as an individual, and his conduct as
a member

a member of fociety. Man, in order to become
a good member of fociety, muſt be inſpired with
religious principles ; that he may not coũnteract
the common views, out of ſecret fraud, malice,
or ſelfiſhneſs, but be carried on to every generous exertion by which the public happineſs can
be effected. Religion, then, muſt enter into
every plan that has the general good or profit in
view. As far, therefore, as we reſpect the
proſperity of our country, we muſt wiſh to extend the influence of religion to all thoſe who
are comprehended within her laws. But, as
Chriſtians, we have ſtill a ſtronger principle of
action to excite us to exert ourſelves in enlarging
the empire of religion by every benevolent method within our power. Religion determines
the future lot of the individual, and the grand
principle of benevolence that runs through it,
makes his happineſs depend on his doing all the
good in his power here to his brethren around
him. But the inſtruction of our negroe ſlaves
is an act of goodneſs of the higheſt and moſt
extenſive nature : and the circumſtances of our
having originally inſlaved them, of their living
intirely for, and depending on us, and too frequently being oppreſſed and cruelly treated by
individuals among us, gives them the ſtrongeſt
claim for receiving it at our hands. The privileges of Chriſtianity are of a diffuſive nature,
and have this condition among others annexed,

that

that we fhall communicate them; freely we have received, freely we muft give. And, in a çafe where none within our reach are to be excepted from fharing in the benefit, how highly incumbent is it on us to exalt to reafon and religion thofe whom our avarice has depreffed, even to brutality.

But, becaufe, in the demand of duty we are often defirous of compounding matters, and in the prefent cafe, probably, may imagine that the higheft purpofes of religion may be gained without fuch an alteration in the condition of flaves, as while it refts on fpeculative arguments, may be thought fomewhat dangerous; it will be neceffary to fhew, that, as the oppreffed fituation of negroe flaves prevents the community from reaping many important advantages from them, fo it incapacitates them from making, in any confiderable degree, a progrefs in religious knowledge. To make a man capable of religion, we muft endow him with the rights and privileges of a man; we muft teach him to feel his weight in fociety, and fet a value on himfelf, as a member of the community, before we can attempt to perfuade him to lay in his claim to heaven. To fhew the reader, therefore, the neceffity of advancing the flave, in the fcale of focial life, before we offer him a participation of our religion, I fhall relate the little efficacy of fuch attempts as have been made to communi-

cate

cate religious knowledge to him in his hitherto debafed ftate. And if fuch a communication be, as I have affirmed, not only a valuable but an indifpenfable objeÆ to fociety, I fhall, in doing this, eftablifh the neceffity of improving his condition in focial life.

S E C T. I.

Examples of the Difficulty found in inftructing Slaves in their prefent State.

I AM forry to be obliged to remark how little, till within thefe very few years, has been attempted or propofed on this head. For though the race of authors and projeÆors equal the leaves of the trees as much in their numbers, as they refemble them in the fhortnefs of their exiftence; yet, unlefs we take into account a few unconneÆed attempts, a few general ftric-túres, and fome unmeaning declamations, our flaves had hardly found a proteÆor worthy of the appellation, till the publication of the late Hiftory of Jamaica; and·the vindication they have found in it, as we fhall have occafion to remark, is on fuch humiliating terms, as will, I fear, do them little good. Still the nature and iffue of thefe attempts to inftruÆ and ferve them in their prefent oppreffed ftate, will be fufficient to mark that improbability of fuccefs which we have affirmed.

Robertfon,

Robertſon, a miniſter in Nevis, about fifty years ago, wrote profeſſedly on the converſion of ſlaves in our colonies, and ſeems to have been willing to have laboured honeſtly in it himſelf. But it is to be remarked of him, that he takes no notice of the intire want of law to ſecure to them proper treatment, nor ſo much as hints that this want is of any diſadvantage to them. And, in reſpeƈt of their converſion, he plainly ſhews that nothing conſiderable can be done in it, unleſs government interpoſe in earneſt to carry it on. But before government can meddle with ſlaves, it muſt take them firſt within the boſom of ſociety, advance their condition, proteƈt in them the claims of human nature, and make them objeƈts of police.

He propoſes that government ſhould keep up a number of miſſionaries among the colonies, by rotation, whoſe whole employment ſhould be to inſtruƈt the ſlaves, as faſt as they acquired the language, or grew up to be capable of inſtruƈtion. Their only reward, he thinks, ſhould be a preſent maintenance, and a promiſe of being provided for at home, when the time of their miſſion was expired. In this plan, the reader will immediately obſerve, that the miſſionary will require ſome time to gain a facility in teaching, and that, if he returns home after a few years, he muſt reſign to others his ſtation, when

when he is become fit to hold it. The time of his employment will, therefore, require to be regulated in a particular manner to obviate this inconveniency.

He earneftly endeavours to exculpate the planters for having done fo little in this affair, from their hurry of bufinefs, their own ignorance, their inability in point of fortune. He farther attempts to prove, that negroes, in general, are ill adapted for inftruction, by reafon of their fulkinefs, ftupidity, prejudices; in many, an incapacity of making any tolerable progrefs in the language ; and, laftly the univerfal carelefineſs that prevails among them about every thing that does not ftrike their fenfes.

In ſhort, from his obfervations, a man would be apt to conclude, that he was of opinion that the manufacture of fugar, and the practice of religion, were things incompatible ; and that before we began to deliberate about the converfion of flaves, the previous queftion had need to be difcuffed, whether we fhould maintain this manufacture, or apply ourfelves to promote the growth of Chriftianity. But whatever may be the intrinfic merit of his plan, it has been too long before the public unnoticed, for us to expect much from it at this day.

A planter

A planter of ———, a man of education,
and of a religious turn of mind, about twenty-
four years ago attempted the converfion of his
own flaves. He himfelf became their catechift
and preacher. He increafed their allowance of
food, clothed them decently, treated them with
humanity, tried to reafon rather than whip
them out of their faults, and granted them many
indulgencies in the hours and degrees of their
labour. He purfued his plan during a good
many years, and, as was faid, at firft with fome
degree of fuccefs: but fome time before his
death, according to the author's information,
he gave up the defign, in defpair of effecting
any thing confiderable by it. The caufes of
his ill fuccefs, that have been affigned, were a
relaxation of difcipline refpecting their obedience
and labour, for which they were not ripe; and
his infifting on too accurate an obfervation of
the fabbath, in the manner of the Jews, while,
they had no mental employment to fubftitute on
it for their ufual private labour, and focial
amufements. In fhort, the indulgencies that
fhould have been the *reward* of improvement
and good behaviour, were made to *precede* them,
and there was nothing left to allure them, or
encourage them in the work. But, fince his
death, feveral of his people have joined themfelves to the Moravians, who have a miffion in
the colony. •

A con-

A confiderable number of years ago, the abfent owner of a plantation fent out pofitive ftanding inftructions to his manager, to have his flaves carefully inftructed in the Chriftian religion, and baptized. He accompanied this order with directions to treat them in every refpect with confiderate humanity, and to do for them whatever was poffible to make their ftate eafy, and their lives happy. The minifter of the parifh accordingly was applied to, and a recompence · for his trouble was agreed on. Here then was a profpect of a fair trial of what could poffibly be effected among flaves in their prefent ftate; but the manager's injudicious choice of an inftructor blafted every reafonable expectation. The minifter was not even oftenfibly decent, and never affected to be guided by principles of duty that he did not feel. He faw nothing in the propofal but an increafe of income to himfelf, and was determined to intitle himfelf to it in the eafieft manner poffible. The following was his method :

He came to the plantation on a Sunday afternoon, and defired the manager to collect eight or ten flaves to be baptized. They were brought before him. He began to repeat the office of baptifm. When he had read as far as that part of the fervice where he was to fprinkle them with water, if their former name pleafed him he baptifed them by it; but if he thought

it

it not fit to call a Chriftian by, as was his opinion
of Quamina, Bungee, and the like, he gave them
the firft Chriftian name which occurred to his
memory. This name the bearer, perhaps,
could not repeat, and fcarcely ever remembered
afterwards ; fo that he continued to be diftinguifhed among his fellows by his old heathen
name.

The minifter, being once afked, what end he
propofed in performing the ceremony in this
fuperficial manner ? he frankly replied, " He
" was paid for doing it ; it did the creatures
" no harm ; and when they died, he fhould
" be paid for burying them." Accordingly the
manager compounded the matter with him,
and gave him yearly a cafk of rum worth about
£ 8 fterling, in lieu of furplus fees due for burying them. He had alfo a falary of £ 20 for
vifiting and praying with the fick, which,
without being earned, he punctually received.
For the baptifms, he was paid a certain fum.

Some of the baptized would mutter, and
fay, they defired not the parfon to throw water
in their face ; which is all that they knew of the
matter, and therefore were loth to fuffer themfelves to be fo dealt with. In fhort, if merely
the making of them parties to a rite that they
underftand not, and in which they take no active
or rational fhare, doth initiate them into Chrift's
church,

church, then are they right good Chriftians. But if fome fhare of knowledge, if fome degree of affent be neceffary to give the minifter's conning over the office of baptifm before them, fome religious effect among them, thefe flaves can pretend to little Chriftianity.   For here the plea of infant baptifm cannot be admitted, becaufe neither non-age nor after-inftruction can be pretended.   In this manner was unfufpecting piety impofed on, and fuch formerly were the minifters recommended for the colonies.

S E C T.   II.

The Obftacles that the Moravian Miffions have to ftruggle with.

THE Moravians fhew a remarkable and laudable degree of affiduity in making converts; and, taking their difficulties into account, they have had, on the whole, no inconfiderable fuccefs.   Their difciples in Antigua are about two thoufand in number; the fruits of twenty years labour.   Several planters encourage their endeavours among their people.   But fome years ago they received a rude fhock from an attempt of a particular mafter to intrude on them Mr. Lindfay's tenets, which required their own firmnefs, and the affection of their converts to defeat.   There are ufually three miffionaries. They have introduced decency and fobriety among

among their people, and no mean degree of religious knowledge. They have infant miffions in Barbadoes, St. Chriftopher's and Jamaica. †

They have made the greateft progrefs in the Danifh colonies. In St. Croix they have fixed a bifhop, with feveral minifters and catechifts under him. They have chapels in the different quarters of the ifland. Many gentlemen have private chapels for their ufe, and encourage them in their labours. Government countenances them; but the Danifh clergymen in the ifland do not favour or affift them.

Every evening, except on Saturday, they have diftinct meetings, by turns, for their baptized and catechumens. Their hour of general worfhip is on Sunday evening; the flaves being obliged to labour on that day for their fubfiftence. The converts are taught to ufe private devotions. When they go to, and leave off work, they fing in concert a few hymns drawn up in the common language. Singing makes a confiderable part of their common worfhip.

The moft fenfible, of both fexes, are raifed to the dignity of elders or helpers, to fuperintend each

† Every thing here faid concerning the fuccefs of the Moravians, and the good effects of it upon the flaves in Antigua, has been lately confirmed to me by a gentleman who has fpent many years in that ifland. But he adds, that the number of negroe converts, inftead of 2000, is upward of 6000.

each the behaviour of their fex, and to
forward the work of inftruction. When a
brother commits a fault, he is mildly reproved
in private, or if it be of a public nature, before
the congregation : if he obftinately perfifts in
the fault, he is, for a time, deprived of the
euchariſt, or feparated from the congregation.
This difcipline feldom fails to produce repentance, on which he is readily re-admitted to the
privileges of the fociety.

In bringing them on in religious knowledge,
they begin by drawing their attention particularly to the fufferings and crucifixion of our
Saviour.   When this is found to have made an
impreffion on their minds, and filled their hearts
with grateful fentiments, they then make them
connect it with repentance and a good life.
Submiffion to their mafters, and full obedience
to their commands, even to working in the plantation, when fo ordered, on Sundays, are ftrongly
inforced ; or rather, they imprefs on them the
neceffity of fubmitting to thofe irregularities
which, in their ftate of fubjection, they cannot
avoid, that their mafters may have no complaint
againft them, while labouring to gain the great
point of general improvement.   Their greateft
trouble arifes from the libidinous behaviour of
overfeers among the female difciples, which,
however, fome mafters check as much as lies
in their power.

The

The great fecret of the miffionary's management, befides foliciting the grateful attention of their hearers to our Saviour's fufferings, is to contract an intimacy with them, to enter into their little interefts, to hear patiently their doubts and complaints, to condefcend to their weaknefs and ignorance, to lead them on flowly and gently, to. exhort them affectionately, to avoid carefully magifterial threatenings and commands.

The confequences of this method are obferved to be a confiderable degree of religious knowledge, an orderly behaviour, a neatnefs in their perfons and clothing, a fobriety in their carriage, a fenfibility in their manner, a diligence and faithfulnefs in their ftations, induftry and method in their own little matters, an humility and piety in their converfation; an univerfal unimpeached honefty in their conduct.

The brethren in Europe are at the expence of the miffionary's journeys, and contribute to their maintenance. They have a fmall plantation in one of the Danifh iflands, from which they draw part of their fupport. Some of the miffionaries, at their leifure hours, apply to mechanic employments. The reft of their fimple maintenance arifes from trifling voluntary collections among their difciples. Some of them are men of learning, others fimple well-meaning men. Their

Their bifhop is a man of plain good fenfe and difcretion.

This account of the Moravians appears, at firft fight, to contradict my pofition, that the prrefent debafed ftate of flaves favours not religious improvem ent.   The circumftances in their favour are, that they are feen by their fcholars only as inftructors or comforters; that they try to lofe fight of flavery and its confequences, and fhew their converts to themfelves only in the light of a religious fociety; that, as far as the fimplicity of their rites will permit, they draw imagination to their affiftance, and paint religion almoft in fenfible colours.

But it may be obferved, that the authority of the mafter which they muft inforce, and the law of God, which they profefs to teach, muft often draw the hefitating flave different ways, and fill his mind with doubt, which of the two is to be obeyed.   God fets apart the fabbath to recruit the body for labour, and improve the mind for futurity; the mafter, having feized for himfelf the work of the week, obliges the flave to toil on that day for his own maintenance; nay, not unfrequently for his (the mafter's) avarice.   Doubtlefs, however it may fare with the profane mafter, the fate of the fiave himfelf is in the beft hands; but he can acquire only an inferior kind of religion, and he he muſt hold even that at the caprice of one who, in himſelf, perhaps has no religion. A mitigation therefore of their ſlavery, and a communication of ſome ſocial privileges, are ſtill a neceſſary foundation for any eminent degree of religious improvement.

S E C T.   III.

Inefficacy of the Author's private Attempts to inſtruct Slaves.

Though ſome individuals may treat their ſlaves with humanity and diſcretion, yet we can give very few inſtances of any attention ſhewn to their *moral improvement,* or of any pains taken to enable them to become partakers of the goſpel promiſes.   Religion is not deemed neceſſary to qualify a ſlave to anſwer any purpoſe of ſervitude ; and while we wiſh them to be diligent and faithful, we never think of placing a monitor within their breaſts, nor of directing them to look up to God, as the obſerver or rewarder of integrity.   Indeed, in the relation of maſter and ſlave, there is ſo little of what is reciprocal in the duty on one ſide and advantage on the other, that it is hardly poſſible to infuſe any other principle than fear into the mind of a ſlave, or to make him conſider himſelf in any other light than that of an unwilling inſtument of his maſter's tyranny and grandeur: a condition that

leaves

leaves him at liberty to feize every opportunity of making his fervice of as little ufe as he can to his mafter, and of making up for the pinching ill treatment that he receives from him, by pilfering and purloining whatever lies open to him.

When the author firft fettled in the Weft-Indies, he freely and openly blamed the carelefInefs of the inhabitants in a matter of this importance, and he refolved within himfelf to fhew how much might be done by one who was in earneft. His flaves were well clothed and plentifully fed; their employment, which was only the common work of a private family, was barely fufficient for the exercife neceffary to preferve their health. There was more than a fufficient number of them. In fhort, they were plump, healthy, and in fpirits. In the evening they were called in, and made to repeat the creed, the Lord's prayer, and a few other prayers that were reckoned beft adapted to them. Their duty was explained to them in terms let down, as much as poffible, to their apprehenfion. Their fears, their hopes, their gratitude, were all made to intereft themfelves in the fubject. They were not punifhed for one fault in ten that they committed, and never with feverity. They were carefully attended when fick. Nothing was at any time required of them but what was neceffary, and much within their ability. But the treatment may
be

be collected from this circumftance; that in eighteen years, though they had been gradually increafing by births and purchafe from ten to twenty in number, not one had died in his family, except infants during the period of nurfing. In other refpects he cannot boaft greatly of his fuccefs.

The firft flave he poffeffed was a French negroe boy, who could tell his beads, and repeat his Pater-nofter. He was placed out in town with a barber: there he formed fuch acquaintances, and acquired fuch habits of idlenefs, as made him a moft irreclaimable run-a-way; and forced his mafter to difpofe of him at a lofs of twenty-four pounds fterling. He hired a fenfible, induftrious, elderly negroe, who feemed well pleafed with his fituation, till he found that he was obliged to attend in the evening at prayers. He plainly faid, he did not love fuch things, and that he, a negroe, had nothing to do with the prayers of white people; and, in a fhort time, he left his place without affigning any other reafon.

He has been obliged to fend three negroes off the ifland for theft and running away, that he might not be under the neceffity of punifhing with feverity. One of them, a fenfible accomplifhed negrefs, was returned on his hands from the Danifh ifland of St. Croix, for being fuch

H   a thief,

a thief, that no body would, venture to take her
into their family. Her own account was different. She had been returned by him, to whom
fhe had been fent down, becaufe his favourite
Sultana had become jealous of her attractions.
To the accufations of theft, fhe replied, that
whatever fhe might formerly have done in her
mafter's family, fhe knew better than to fteal
in an ifland, where, for taking the leaft trifle,
fhe might, without noife, have been taken up,
and executed immediately. She concluded,
that her being fent back alive was a demon-
ftration of her not having been guilty of theft
during her exile. He was obliged to affect a
fatisfaction in her defence. And, though by
no means faultlefs, yet, either from partial reformation, (for fhe was very capable of reafoning) or an unwillingnefs to make another
trip from her native country, fhe continued to
behave more carefully and attentively in the family ; and at laft became fo induftrious as to
be able to buy out her own, and a daughter's
freedom, that fhe had by a free-man. But he
poffeffed not a fingle flave on whom he could
place dependence. And, had it not been for a
white woman, whofe employment was to watch
them, and whofe care he ufed, as others do
correction, to keep them from difhonefty, he
would have been at a lofs how to have carried
on houfe-keeping, without a degree of feverity

rity abhorrent to his temper. Now, while they continued abandoned, irreclaimable, and infenfible of good treatment, they could be very little difpofed to become Chriftians.

From this unfavourable view of his flaves, it muft not be concluded, that all are abfolutely worthlefs. You often meet with a flave attached to his mafter's intereft, and in moft refpects truft-worthy. The author knows fome that would not lofe, on comparifon, with the moft circumfpect and faithful fervants in Britain. Slaves, indeed, are frequently attached to the perfons of their mafters, and will rifk their lives readily for them, who yet make very free with their property. To fpeak generally, thofe mafters are beft ferved, who feed and clothe their flaves well, who are themfelves methodical in their bufinefs, and never take notice of a fault in them unlefs they mean to correct them fmartly for it. *They* are *ill* ferved, who are carelefs in their manner, indifferent how they are treated, averfe to or irregular in their method of chaftifement. And can any behaviour different from this be expected in creatures, whofe only motive of action is prefent feeling, who have no reputation to fupport, no lafting intereft to care for?

The author is fenfible that his want of fuccefs was, in a certain degree, owing to a want

of

of ſtrictneſs in the method of treating his ſlaves, adapted to their preſent debaſed ſtate. And this aroſe equally from his want of reſolution to perſevere in the diſagreeable work, and from the ſituation of his family, a private one not methodically and conſtantly employed in particular buſineſs. This circumſtance rendered it incapable of being regulated with the accuracy of a plantation, where every hour has its employment, and every piece of work its overſeer. Nor are any families among us ſo well regulated as thoſe connected with plantations, where method in correction and work makes ſome amends for the want of principle in our manner of managing ſlaves. This, at firſt view, may appear harſh to the humane and pious; but it is not, therefore, the leſs a true picture of human nature; nor to thoſe who are acquainted with the neceſſity and effects of diſcipline in our army and navy, will it reflect any particular diſgrace on the natural bias or capacity of Africans. Human nature, wherever found in the ſame debaſed ſtate, would ſhew itſelf in the ſame worthleſs manner. Nor is it an argument for ſtraitening, but for relaxing, and at laſt entirely breaking, the chain of ſlavery.

Maſter and ſlave are in every reſpect oppoſite terms; the perſons to whom they are applied, are natural enemies to each other. Slavery,

very, in the manner and degree that it exifts in our colonies, could never have been intended for the focial ftate ; for it fuppofes tyranny on one fide, treachery and cunning on the other. Nor is it neceffary to difcufs which gives firft occafion to the other. But as flavery has over-run fo large a portion of fociety, the beft thing now to be done, is to prefs its neceffary ftrid̂-nefs of difcipline into the fervice of freedom. In conformity to this reafoning, I affirm, that, If ever the reformation, of which we intend to treat, takes place, it muft begin in *a plantation*, where forms, that are the firft traces, the out-lines of rationality can be accurately afcertain-ed, and conftantly enforced, by perfevering me-thod and difcipline. The mild and argumenta-tive Solon could regulate the fprightly, fenfible Athenians; but the rough, unfeeling Ruffians required a Draco, in their Peter the Great, to wreft their brutality from them. In our cafe, the block muft, in fome meafure be chipt in the rude manner of this laft, before the light touches of the polifher can take effed̂.*

The

* In this, and every other place, where a ftrefs is laid on forms and difcipline, the reader is defired to diftinguifh be-tween ftrid̂nefs and cruelty. What is here fuggefted, is point-ed at the mafter, more than the flave, and intends nothing violent or abrupt. If the mafter be exad̂, and careful in his own duty, he will have little reafon to complain of the flave. Exad̂nefs of method prevents faults, and cuts off the neceffity of punifhment. It is the ignorant, the immethodical, the
negligent,

The author cannot, indeed, fatisfy himfelf with what he has done, and continues to do, in fpite of difappointment. The thing when confidered by itfelf, appears fo plaufible, and mild treatment makes in his imagination, fo amiable a part of it, that he is ready to hope, he has only miffed the right road, and may be more fuccefsful, if he could ftrike out a new plan. Again, when it is confidered, how much the negroes are immerfed in fenfe, how their intellectual powers are wholly employed in the fervice of the body, and that, refpecting them, we have accefs to the firft only by methods that make impreffion on the other; when he revolves the difficulty of managing, by argu-ment alone, a few flaves living and having their connections among hundreds of their equals, who are reftrained only by the whip, every hope of governing them, without a certain de-gree of difcipline, fubfides; he is reduced to barely wifhing, and praying, that things were otherwife than he has found them, after his beft endeavours.

The example and converfation of our equals, will ever have greater influence on our beha-viour,

negligent, the gadding manager, or overfeer, who muft make up for all his own defects by ftripes, and cruel ufage to thofe who are under him. In Chap. I. Sect. 7, we gave an inftance of great ftrictnefs of difcipline, without the ufual proportion of punifhment. Four times out of five the flave is punifhed for the overfeer's fault.

viour, than the precepts or example of thofe who are fuppofed to be under other laws, and to have their lives regulated by rules different from thofe that we think are appointed for us. And it may be prefumed, that the eafy treatment which made part of the author's fcheme, be-caufe moft agreeable to his difpofition, produced in minds not capable of diftinguifhing lenity from want of power, that carelefnefs to pleafe, and pronenefs to ill behaviour, which marked his fmall number of flaves.

This was the cafe of the author's flaves, and the reafoning about them, as matters ftood in the year 1771. Since the dreadful hurricane of 1772, which fwept away all their little ftock, there has been fome change for the better in their general conduct. They have taken a turn to induftry in their own little concerns, which has given them a relifh for property (a turn that fhould always be encouraged) and this has had an effect on their behaviour. In confe-quence of this, the greateft part of them have been admitted to baptifm, and were not the mafter too frequently obliged to interpofe in matters of domeftic concern, to check that fpirit of carelefnefs and oppofition, which naturally rifes againft the views of authority, the ca-techift and teacher might have appeared to have made fome confiderable progrefs among them. Though the relaxed difcipline of the family made

made them ftill rather carelefs of pleafing, yet
they kept more at home, and behaved more
honeftly ; and while fome feemed attached
through principle, all had become more decent
and orderly than in the former period.

But though they were flaves only in name,
except in the not being at liberty to change
the place of their abode at pleafure, and though
become more manageable than before, yet the
reluctance that run through and affected the
fervice of the beft, with only one exception ;
the biafs they had to the manners and company of the flaves around them ; the neceffity
of following them up in every ftep of duty impofed on them, and of keeping the fear of
punifhment fufpended over them; in fhort, the
apparent uneafinefs on one fide, and the indifpenfable miftruft on the other, plainly
proved that they had no folid enjoyment of
themfelves. And indeed it was the ftrong feeling he had of thefe difficulties in the management of his flaves, which principally contributed
to make the fituation of their mafter moft irkfome to him, and to render a ftate of affluence
and eafe, (in a fettlement otherwife as agreeable
as imagination can well paint) fo difguftful, as
induced him with eagernefs to embrace the
firft opportunity that a generous friendfhip offered, of a retreat in a country, in which,
though lefs favourable to his health, and the
views

views of his family, he could indulge the feelings of benevolence without regret.

SECT. IV.

Inefficacy of the Author's Public Attempts to inftruct Slaves.

ON his firft fettlement as a minifter in the Weft-Indies, he made alfo fome *public* attempts to inftruct flaves. He began to draw up fome eafy, plain difcourfes for their inftruction. He invited them to attend on Sundays, at particular hours. He appointed hours at home, to inftruct fuch fenfible flaves as would of themfelves attend. He repeatedly exhorted their mafters to encourage fuch in their attendance. He recommended the French cuftom, of beginning and ending work by prayer. But inconceivable is the liftleffnefs with which he was heard, and bitter was the cenfure heaped on him in return. It was quickly fuggefted, and generally believed, that he wanted to interrupt the work of flaves, to give them time, forfooth, to fay their prayers; that he aimed at the making of them Chriftians, to render them incapable of being good flaves. In one word, he ftood, in opinion, a rebel convict againft the intereft and majefty of planterfhip. And as the Jews fay, that in every punifhment, with which they have been proved, fince the bondage of Egypt, there has been an ounce of the golden calf of Horeb; fo may he fay, that in

H 5   every

every inftance of prejudice (and they have not been a few) with which, till within a year or two of his departure from the country, he has been exercifed, there has been an ounce of his fruitlefs attempts to improve the minds of flaves.

No mafter would ufe any influence with his flaves, to make them attend at the appointed hours. Even fome, who approved of the plan, or at leaft durft not, for fhame, objeɛt to it, and who would have been offended with the man that fhould have infinuated their difregard to religion, did not think themfelves obliged to co-operate, or encourage their flaves to attend on inftruɛtion. Nor did this backwardnefs proceed from a dread of the ill confequences of improvement, but from an indolence in fuch matters, that cannot be explained to one unacquainted with the country.

In the bidding prayer, he had inferted a petition for the converfion of flaves. It was deemed fo difagreeable a memento, that feveral white people, on account of it, left off attending divine fervice. He was obliged to omit the prayer entirely, to try and bring them back. In fhort, neither were the flaves, at that time, defirous of being taught, nor were their mafters inclined to encourage them. But as this refers to a period about eighteen years ago, which, in change of inhabitants, is there equal to a generation,

neration, there is ground to hope that the ancient prejudices againſt the converſion of the negroes may, ſince that æra, in ſome iſlands and in ſome plantations, be a good deal abated.

SECT. V.

The Manner ſuggeſted, in which private Attempts on large Plantations, to improve Slaves, may probably ſucceed.

LITTLE, we ſee, can be ſaid of the endeavours of individuals, within the author's knowledge, to improve their ſlaves. Some years ago he ſcarce knew a man on the ſpot, who had ſeriouſly attended to their inſtruction, or who believed that intereſt, duty, or reputation, obliged him to attempt it. Nay, though the more moderate and ſenſible people allow that the inſtruction of ſlaves, if their preſent condition permitted it, and it could be brought about, would be a good thing, yet it is not to be concealed, that ſome have ſtrong objections againſt every meaſure that has their benefit in view, or that conſiders them in any other light than inſtruments of labour. An owner will, indeed, ſometimes have a favourite ſlave baptized; but I am not ſenſible of any care having been taken, either before or after, with one in ten, who are indulged with the rite, to ſee that they be inſtructed.

I was

I was once requeſted to baptize a negreſs, remarkable for her faithfulneſs and attachment to her owner's intereſt. On examination, I found her grofsly ignorant, and unuſually inattentive. In the eaſieſt manner in my power I attempted to inſtruct her, and as ſhe lived in the neighbourhood, bid her come frequently to me. I ſpoke alſo to her owners, mentioned her ignorance, and expreſſed my readineſs to inſtruct her. She never attended, was carried into another pariſh, and there baptized, I had almoſt ſaid, without ceremony. Baptiſm is ſuppoſed to free a ſlave from the power of the negroe conjurer, and its being permitted, is confidered, in the maſter, as the conferring of a favour that is complete, when the rite is performed. The lot of ſlaves, reſpecting religion, is moſt favourable, when they happen to be preſented young to a growing up daughter of the family, or to be the property of induſtrious people, juſt above the loweſt rank. In theſe caſes, care is ſometimes taken to fit them for baptiſm, and ſome turn out tolerably ſober, and ſenſible; but their proportion to the whole can hardly be taken into account.

But if ſlaves in *their preſent ſtate* be capable of any *conſiderable* improvement, it will probably be on large plantations, where they compoſe communities of themſelves, and where the diſcipline neceſſary for humanizing them can be carried on with the greateſt ſtrictneſs and effect.

effect. In this point of view is the following plan propofed.

In the firft place, a chaplain muft be appointed; and a man of confiderable affiduity would find full employment among the ufual numbers, that extenfive plantations contain of fuch ignorant creatures. If a fober difcreet man in orders could be found, who underftood phyfic enough to enable him to take charge of their fick, greater encouragement could be given, and one office would promote the other. For both, a fingle man fhould be allowed £250 fterling per annum, the ufe of an horfe and a boy, and board with the manager. No man, acquainted with the country, will confider this appointment as exceffive, for a man of a liberal education.

The chaplain fhould teach the flaves fome fhort prayers, to be repeated by them in private, when they rife in the morning, and when they go to fleep. He fhould accuftom them to repeat fome fhort inftructive form refpecting their focial duties, when they begin and leave off their field work. The black overfeers, as in the French colonies, may foon be taught to take the lead in their field devotions.

A chapel fhould be built for the performance of divine fervice on Sunday, for prayers on the days when their allowance of provifions is diftributed,

tributed, for celebrating the offices of matrimony and baptifm, and any other occafion of
meeting together.   A burying ground fhould be
fet apart for the decent interment of the dead,
and it fhould be allotted out according to their
families.   It would have an excellent effect on
them, if only tractable, well-difpofed perfons
were buried with their families, and every
worthlefs fellow buried in a place apart.

The chapel fhould be built near the hofpital, that all, who are under cure, may, if able,
attend fervice. The chaplain fhould be inftant
in inftructing thofe in the hofpital, that his
teaching may interefere the lefs with their ordinary work in health. And as a confiderable proportion, on fome account or other, will be
received into the hofpital within the year,
fomething valuable may be effected by embrac-
ing that opportunity.   By applying particularly
to bring forward the more fenfible and teachable flaves, he may enable them in time to
affift him in the work, and by little rewards,
which he may be allowed to beftow, he may
fecure their help ; but efpecially, he may give
the parents affection a turn to the inftruction
of their children. The great difficulty will
be, to let down the language of religion to
their prefent capacity : a convincing proof with
me, that however flavery may be permitted,
yet originally Providence never defigned any
rational, . or accountable creature for fuch a
deprefled brutifh ftate, as that of African flaves

in

in the Britifh colonies. But if a few were once well-grounded in religious knowledge, they could talk more familiarily and feelingly to their fellows, than the minifter; and his chief bufinefs, except general inftruction, would then be to fuperintend their conduct, and excite them to the work. The young children generally fhew themfelves four or five times a day in a gang, with fmall parcels of grafs, picked for the cattle. They may be made to repeat fome fhort general precept, on delivering in their bundles, the moft forward boy taking the lead.

Sundays are ufually fpent by induftrious flaves, in their own provifion grounds. To give them time for improvement and devotion on that day, they muft be allowed at leaft Saturday afternoon for their own work; taking care to keep them honeftly employed, that they may not go robbing, or ftealing, or get into drunken brawls. Few, at firft, could bear fuch indulgence, without ftrict looking after.

As the manager will object to a regulation that curtails the working hours of his people, to induce him to allow the flaves this time, he muft be permitted to make up for the labour reduced in giving up Saturday afternoon to themfelves, by adding gradually to the gang, on a large plantation, about thirty young negroes. If the owner fhould, from delicacy,

obje.

object to the buying of flaves, perhaps the confideration of its producing a benefit to the whole, may prevail on him. This would be an expence at firft, but, by increafing the vigour and induftry of the flaves, would in time improve his property greatly beyond their firft coft. And as the flaves might be made to perform their own work, under the direction of the overfeers, their patches of ground would be better cultivated, and give greater increafe, than when each is left to work as he pleafeth. This is on the fuppofition, that fuch plantations, are fully ftocked for the prefent views of the proprietors.

The gang fhould be marfhalled by families, each divifion being put under the care of the principal perfon in it, who fhould be anfwerable for their conduct. At ftated times they fhould pafs in review, be examined in refpect of health, give an account of their clothes, and the feveral articles of their little property. Then fhould follow an inquiry into their religious progrefs, and a diftribution of rewards among the moft diligent, either in getting themfelves, or their children and fellows forward. Much would depend on the temper and difcretion of the minifter; much on the hearty concurrence of the manager.

A large public thatched room fhould be built, in which to hold their feafts and merry-makings;

makings; and the man of the greateft influence and fobriety among them, fhould be chofen by themfelves, and approved of by the manager, to be mafter of the revels, and keep them harm-lefs and within bounds. Some folemn act of prayer, or thankfgiving, fhould begin and end every affembly.

No offence, except infolence and difobedi-ence, fhould be punifhed by the manager, till it has been fubmitted to the decifion of a jury, chofen from among themfelves. This would accuftom them to mark the difference between right and wrong, and at leaft make confiderate and prudent flaves fhun faults, which they had condemned in their neighbour's practice. All punifhments fhould be inflicted with folemnity, in prefence of the gang, accompanied with fome fhort explanation of the crime, and an exhortation from the chaplain, to abftain from it. Infolence and difobedience are left to be punifhed at the difcretion of the manager, till the flaves become capable of moral government, becaufe he would not be able to fupport his authority, if obliged to fubmit the difcuffion of faults committed againft himfelf, to the deci-fion of other perfons.

It is difficult to determine what reformation this example, and the good effects produced by this extraordinary care, might produce in a neighbourhood. But judging from analogy, we muft muſt not expect the fruits to be of a very quick growth, or very ſpreading nature. Thus, for inſtance, we know that intereſt pleads equally with humanity, for the kind treatment of ſlaves. Every diſcreet man feelingly acknowledges it; yet how often, in practice, do theſe principles ſeem to be at variance, in ſpite of the moſt convincing example which their union, in men of prudence and ſentiment, can produce? How frequently may intereſt, or rather her accurſed phantom, ſelfiſhneſs, be ſeen dragging a human creature in a chain, naked, ſtarved, and raw with ſtripes, and demanding, with threats, that tale of labour, which cruelty has rendered the wretch incapable of performing?

Now if example be ſo little of a diffuſive nature, in a caſe ſuch as this, in which all conſider themſelves as concerned, what may we expect to happen in religion, which is not deemed the concern of any particular perſon? The liſtleſſneſs in ſuch matters is too univerſal; the deſire of preſent gain too general, for any conſiderable proportion of the inhabitants to fall ſuddenly and eagerly into a ſcheme, that promiſes ſo little immediate profit, and ſeems to be ſo very foreign to their buſineſs, or duty, and ſo far above the capacity of the objects of this improvement. *

Yet

* Among the ancients, not only the fine arts, but ſciences and philoſophy, in particular inſtances, were cultivated by ſlaves. Theſe were therefore immediate objects of religion

and

Yet on no account is there reafon to defpair. Good fenfe would induce the imitation of fome ; religion, awakened by confcience, would exert her influence with others ; fhame would oblige many, vanity more; the natural progrefs of knowledge and reafon in the human mind, though flow to anfwer the wifhes of fentiment, would go on gradually to accomplifh the important work. Even among the fenfible flaves, emulation would have great effects. On the whole, the caufe of humanity and religion would be ferved. But whatever might be the iffue with others, were fuch flaves as thefe of whom we treat, advanced in focial life gradually, as they fhewed themfelves capable of improvement, nothing could hinder their mafters from reaping the happieft fruits from their humanity, piety, and good fenfe. They would be more healthy,

and morality. But their fituation differed greatly from that of our African flaves. Thefe are favages ravifhed from their huts, and their country, to till, like brutes, a ftrange foil, in a ftrange climate, among people of a ftrange fpeech, without rights, without privileges, without enjoyments. The ancient flaves were often perfons of condition, deprived of their freedom by the accidents of war ; or fuch as had been liberally brought up in their mafter's family, and looked forward to freedom in his affection or gratitude. Thefe once accuftomed to reflect, purfued their ftudies, and fearched in philofophy, or religion, for fupport under the miferies of their condition. In their cafe, no infolent pride in the mafter, of fuppofing himfelf of an higher race, blocked up the path to their advancement. It is pride with us forms an infeparable bar to every generous wifh. Emulation is frozen ; expectation is dead ; the heavenly fpark lies fmothered in anguifh and neglect, while all around is darknefs and doubt.

healthy, more vigorous, more diligent, more honeſt ; they would riſe in the ſcale of being, poſſeſs
more of the conveniencies of life, enjoy more happineſs, and look forward with more confidence
into futurity.   I have mentioned the neceſſity of
making ſocial privileges, to accompany attempts
at mental improvement, becauſe I am perſuaded,
that little of conſequence can be gained in the
laſt, without beſtowing ſomething proportionably
conſiderable on the other.   But we ſhall leave
the diſcuſſion of this point, to make a part of
our particular plan of improvement. *

In

* That particular points may be gained among ſlaves, in
their preſent ſtate, though we have few examples of *general*
improvement, may be concluded from the following narration.

On a plantation in a tobacco colony, lived ſome years ago
a manager, a German, a reduced army officer. He formed
the ſlaves into a regiment, dividing them into commands, and
appointing officers over them.   Their motions were performed, and their work was regulated by beat of drum. He
planted armed centinels as in a garriſon.   Offences were tried
as in a court martial, and none were puniſhed till their equals
had adjudged them to be guilty. A corporal had deſerted and
carried off his arms. The officer received intelligence of him,
and as it was the firſt inſtance of deſertion, and the offender
had alſo killed one of his companions, it was neceſſary to
make a ſtriking example of it. The officer went at the head
of an armed party, and ſurrounded the houſe where the corporal lay hid. It was night, and happened to be moon-light.
The noiſe ſoon brought the deſerter out, armed with his muſket.
The officer, while advancing on him with his muſket preſented, bid him ſurrender, and on no account to preſent his piece,
for on the ſmalleſt attempt he would ſhoot him; on the other
hand, he aſſured him, on his honour, that he ſhould have a fair
trial. The corporal hoped to command more favourable terms
in a poſture of defence, but in attempting to level his piece,

the

In general we affirm, that the master, or legiſlature, that aims at improvement, or defires to promote good order, muſt keep their people ſtrictly to forms, and make the individuals judges of each other's behaviour. Breaches of morality may, under proper general ſanctions, be left to the unbiaſſed opinions of the people. To direct induſtry, and indifferent habits, to a plan of general utility and obedience, is the object of police. To carry form and method into private life, is the true ſecret to impart firmneſs, both to law and empire.

It was not the *laws* of Lycurgus, which might not be in contemplation once in a man's life, but it was his *cuſtoms*, which met the citizen at every meal, that gave ſtability to Sparta. The decalogue, and the other principles of morality, fill a ſmall ſpace in the laws of Moſes, and reſpect every other nation equally with the Jews; but ablutions, feſtivals, and ſacrifices returned on his people, at every hour; and they were the inſtitutes which have principally ſecured obedience to that conſtitution through a longer period of time, than any other ſyſtem has been

able

the officer ſhot him dead. He was tried in the provincial courts for killing the man, and was acquitted. But to ſhew his people, that he did not make one law for them, and another for himſelf, he had the cauſe formally difcuſſed in his own plantation court, and was unanimouſly abſolved. The effects that would naturally be produced by ſuch a diſcipline, enforced by ſuch an example, muſt, in things to which it is extended, be great and laſting.

able to effect. Man is compofed of matter and intellect; and he who would be mafter of the laft, muft not neglect the culture of the other. Our Englifh laws pafs over the private conduct of the citizens to attend to nuifances, and impofe taxes. Hence that abfurdity of conduct, that inconfiftency, that extravagance of behaviour, that mifapplication of time, and wealth, which prevail among us, above all others, in private life. And yet how can the public carry on that joint purpofe, which is the end of fociety, or how can it flourifh as a community, when individuals are left, each man to follow his own caprice ? *

In

* To give one inftance out of thoufands of this neglect. The fate of the nation is fuppofed to be bound up with trade, yet is every man permitted to finifh his own manufactures in his own way, by which the national character and intereft fuffer daily among foreigners. This might be prevented, by permitting nothing to be exported, till it has endured the fcrutiny of proper judges, and had its quality ftampt on it by authority. This negligence, ere this, would have been as fatal in other branches, as it has already been in the Turkey trade, but for that emulation which naturally arifes among competitors in the fame branches.

This fyftem of directing by authority the private conduct of citizens, was carried a faulty length by the Jefuits in Paraguay. There the individual was confidered as a mere inftrument of public order, and public induftry, without having any thing permitted to his own feelings, or inclination. And our flaves fuffer in proportion, as they are under a mafter, who is more or lefs teafing and difturbing them in their own hours, and little concerns. But furely, it would not be difficult to oblige, by the regulations of police, a man to be happy in himfelf, and to add happinefs to thofe around him, by fixing on the proper medium in managing him, between carelefInefs and inftruction. The difference is exceeding great in our flaves,

when

In short, we have too few circumstances, that bring us together, or oblige us to consider ourselves as members of the same community. The social nature of our religion has indeed hitherto made up for many of the other defects, and prevented us from feeling their ill consequence. But in proportion as the notions of Epicurus become fashionable among us, this tie drops off also, and, in all probability, unless we except our taxes, we shall soon have nothing in common as a people, but the sea that surrounds our isle. A desire of pointing out the way of giving success to the particular attempt here recommended, amidst the difficulties that surround it, has insensibly led to this digression.

when employed for their masters and for themselves. In the first case they drawl their task out, and weep under the burden, listless, and careless of success. See them on a Sunday morning, that only day of liberty, going to market with their own provisions, they walk strong, their faces cheerful, their bodies erect, their persons neat, and the whole man elevated and improved. Now the police that we recommend above, makes the man contribute to the general prosperity, while he imagines himself wholly taken up in pursuing his own interest, and exerting himself in his own business.

C H A P.

C H A P. IV.

Natural Capacity of Slaves vindicated.

To thofe who, with Mofes, believe that all men had one common parent, though for wife ends different families have fince had diftinguifhing marks fixed on them, the fubject of this chapter would be an unneceffary digreffion. But we are fo fond of an hypothefis, which indulges pride, and faves the trouble of enquiry, that the contrary, though leading to nothing generous, though narrow, felfifh, and illiberal, has found powerful advocates, who draw after them crowds of admirers. Therefore, before we proceed to claim the rights of fociety, and of a common religion for Africans, we muft firft put them in poffeffion of that humanity, which is pertinacioufly difputed with them. With this view I fhall confider the objections made to their capacity, from hypothefis, from figure, from anatomy, from obfervation, and prove their natural powers, from reafon and experience.

S E C T. I.

Objections to African Capacity, drawn from Philofophy, confidered.

HUME, in his Effays, broacheth an opinion concerning negroes, which, if true, would render
whatever

whatever could be advanced in their favour, of no account. But I truſt his aſſertion, which certainly was made without any competent knowledge of the ſubject, will appear to have no foundation, either in reaſon or nature. In his Eſſay on National Characters he ſays, " That " mankind is compoſed of three or four different " races ; and that there never was a poliſhed " ſociety, but of the white race, to which all " others are naturally inferior." In particular, he gives it as his formed opinion, " that there " never aroſe a man of genius among negroes."

Had he lived in the days of Auguſtus, or even but a thouſand years ago, his northern pride, perhaps, would have been leſs aſpiring, and ſa-tisfied to have been admitted even on a footing of equality with the ſable Africans. Virgil makes Dido inſinuate to Æneas, the reaſon he had to expect humane treatment among her peo-ple, not becauſe they were poliſhed Phœnicians, but becauſe they dwelt more immedi ately than other powers under the powerful influence of the ſun. And in the time of Charlemagne, a fo-reign divine, writing to the Britons to encourage them, tells them, as a thing remarkable, that though their country lay far " north, yet it " had produced ſeveral great men." Suppoſ-ing theſe, and Hume's obſervations, (if indeed theſe deſerve the name) to have been drawn equally from fact, the concluſion is, that arts, ſciences, and the poliſhed life accompanying

I   them,

them, are flowly progreffive through nations and climates, rather than that the natives of any particular country are born incapable of them in their turn, as if intended to act an inferior part in the moral world.

Again, in his Natural hiftory of Religion, he affirms, that if a traveller found a people void of religion, he would find them removed but few degrees from brutes. † He fays, " In the " progrefs of human thought, the ignorant mul- " titude muft firft entertain fome grovelling " familiar notion of fuperior powers, before " they ftretch their conceptions to that perfect " Being, who beftowed order on the frame of " nature ;" ‡ " to believe," faith he, " invifible, " intelligent

---

† Yet, why, if fuch be the man's genuine fentiments, did he ftrive, in all his writings, to difgrace religion, and deftroy every moral fentiment connected with it among his country-men ? I will not fay what name fuch cool malevolence de-ferves; but, on the other hand, let not his friends pretend to exalt the author of fuch peftilential tenets above every human character.

‡ This is with a view to eftablifh his favourite pofition, that polytheifm was the firft religion : becaufe, he there fays, " Man could not poffibly have degenerated from pure theifm " to polytheifm; and yet, we know, that polytheifm has " prevailed." But, forgetting this impoffibility of degene-racy, in order to fhew the little confequence of religion in general, and, as he humanely and refpectfully obferves, to fet the religious fects a wrangling, while he and a few more choice fpirits are making their efcape into the calm regions of philofophy; he afterwards tells us, that man changes continu-ally

" intelligent power, is a ftamp fet by the divine
" Workman on human nature. Nothing dig-
" nifies man more than to be felected from all
" the other parts of the creation to bear this
" image of the univerfal Creator." Here,
then, we have religion for a badge of excellence
or reafon, and the want of it a mark of inferiority or brutality. Speaking of the white or
fuperior race, he goes on to affirm, that the
bulk of mankind is incapable of being directed by
the tenets of pure theifm ; that all popular reli-
gions, in the conception of their more vulgar
votaries, are therefore, a fpecies of demoniafm ;
and that religious principles as they have prevailed in the world, are only fick mens dreams.

Now, if we affume, as we juftly may, that
a perfection to be found very feldom in a fuperior race, cannot be expected in any inftance in
an inferior race ; according to him, we fhall
in vain look among negroes for what is rare in
the white race. Here and there we fee a man
fix feet in ftature ; but were there fuch a nation
as Fabulifts defcribe pigmies to be, would a
traveller

---

ally from polytheifm to theifm, and from theifm to polytheifm ; and, in his opinion, it is a matter of no confequence.
But confiftency in the apoftle of infidelity is as little neceffary,
as in the lives of thofe for whom the doctrine is calculated.
There, is, indeed, fomething fo degrading in all Hume's philofophy, as can recommend it only to a corrupt heart, and
a vitiated underftanding, which fee nothing to wifh for, or excite their emulation, out of the circle of animal indulgencies.

traveller expect to find a pigmy fix feet tail ? In suppofing a diftinction, we deny to the inferior every mark of excellency that diftinguifhes one indvidual of the fuperior race from his fellows. If, then, his fuppofition be juft, it follows that negroes are not intended for religion. For, whatever be his private fentiments of revealed religion, he muft allow it to be a fpecies of general religion ; and he admits the reception of religion to be a perfection in the fuperior race, an advancement of their nature, that few in comparifon of the whole do really attain unto. He alfo allows that Chriftianity contains many of the fublime truths of theifm, which, according to his opinion, no fociety, even of white men, ever yet lived up to. It would then be abfurd to expect that negroes, an inferior race, fhould be capable of an excellence, even in that lefs degree, fuppofed to be contained in Chriftianity, to which a great proportion of the fuperior race, I will not fay cannot, but do not, attain.

But there is fomething in a well-difpofed mind, that makes the man revolt againft this cruel opinion : and, I truft, nature flatly contradicts the affertion. As far as I can judge, there is no difference between the intellects of whites and blacks, but fuch as circumftances and education naturally produce.

It is true, there are marks, that appear now to be eftablifhed, as if fet by the hand of nature to

diftinguifh

diftinguifh them from the whites : their nofes
are flat, their chins prominent, their hair woolly,
their fkin black. They who, from Mofes believe (and, fince, on any fcheme we muft come
to a particular time when the diftinction took
place, it is, to fay no more, juft as fenfible, as
any other pofition) that the Deity parcelled out
the earth into families and languages, may conclude, that thefe diftinctions gradually took
place at a period in which the fons of men
were conducted by the invifible hand of Providence each to his allotted habitation. And, let
it be remarked, that the characteriftics of negroes
fhew themfelves chiefly about the face, where
nature has fixed both the national attributes and
the difcriminating features of individuals, as if
intended to diftinguifh them from other families,
and bind them in the focial tie with their brethren. But their tongues are as mufical, † their
hands as elegant and apt, their limbs as neatly
turned, and their bodies as well formed for
ftrength and activity as thofe of the white race.

After firft writing the above, I was for a fhort
time

† It is furprizing, that during the continued rage for
Italian fingers, it has never entered among the whims of the
age, to try if mufic might not be imported from the Banks of
the Niger. It is certain the natural tafte of the Africans for
mufic is confiderable ; and inftruction and affiduity might
change mungo's filly ftage gibberifh into the foft thrills and
quavers of Italian eunuchs. By the way, how would it have
hurt the pride of an overweening Hume among the Romans,
to have been told, that the time would come when his fons
fhould be emafculated to fit them for entertaining on a ftage
the barbarous Britons with effeminate mufic?

time made happy, by finding that Lord Kaims, in his firſt volume of Sketches, had indulged the ſuppoſition, that at the diſperſion, on the con-fuſion of languages, when the earth was divided among Noah's poſterity, national attributes firſt took place in the ſeveral families, in the ſeveral climates. But this ſatisfaction continued only till I entered on the peruſal of the ſecond volume : where it is affirmed, that the inhabitants of America have an origin diſtinct from the natives of the eaſtern hemiſphere. We ſhall, therefore, conſider theſe opinions together. *

That

* In a late well known Hiſtory of America there is room to imagine, that the author entertains the ſame opinion with Lord Kaims. He guards it, indeed, by ſaying, that we ſhould be apt to believe the Americans had a different origin, if the ſcriptures did not aſſure us that mankind ſprung from one ſtock. The doctor did not reflect that many of his readers had not the ſame opinion of the ſcriptures as he entertained ; and that his conjecture, as an hiſtorian, would weigh more with them, than his faith as a Chriſtian. He, probably, threw it out as a ſpeculative opinion, without attending to the in-human conſequences deduced from it, and certainly he grounds it on very controvertible data. When he acknow-ledged the apparent difference, he ſhould have been aware of the ſcepticiſm of the age, and guarded againſt the concluſions that would eagerly be drawn from it.

Indeed, the friends of virtue have ſeldom been ſufficiently careful in this reſpect. Before any ſpeculative opinion be given to the world, a man ſhould turn it in his mind every poſſible way, to conſider to what uſes it may be wreſted by infidelity, when brought out under the ſanction of his name. A profeſſed enemy of virtue muſt be placed in particular cir-cumſtances to be able to do much harm in the world by his writings ; but every reverie of an eminent good man is eagerly

ſeized

That without the information afforded by facred hiftory, and without an attention to that extenfive plan of divine œconomy which it opens to us, we fhould, at firft fight, imagine the feveral families inhabiting the earth to have had diftinct progenitors, I readily acknowledge. But, fince a hiftory confiftent in itfelf, uncontradicted by authority, agreeing in analogy with the paft and prefent ftate of things, and fupported by every poffible collateral evidence of hiftory, tradition, national manners, and cuftoms, affures us that men had one common anceftor, that at a period, when men had become numerous, profligate, and daring, their Creator, to punifh their rebellion, and, (conformably to that divine benevolence which conftantly brings good out of evil) to make it inftrumental in advancing fociety, and the more equal and fpeedy cultivation of the earth, divided them into families and languages, giving to each diftinct features, and a feparate fpeech : this, I fay, - being the cafe, we are not left at liberty to purfue every wild conjecture. Both methods, at firft,

feized on, if it can be turned to promote the purpofes of profligacy. Would Locke, even in the eagernefs of difputation, have hazarded that wild conjecture, that poffibly matter might think, could he have forefeen that it would have eftablifhed him as a main pillar of materialifm, and made him anfwerable for all its dreary confequences. In arguing, as in wreftling, we are not fo careful to preferve ourfelves from falling, as anxious to throw our adverfary.

firſt, were equally eaſy to ſupreme power; both, at firſt, ſtood equally in need of an extraᵢ ordinary volition or exertion of Omnipotence. But we can obſerve a peculiar propriety in chooſing the latter. By giving man one ſimple origin, by beſtowing on him a common nature, a foundation was laid for the ultimate re-union of mankind, as well now in improved ſocial life as in futurity ; a re-union intended to take place in time under the then-promiſed connecting head of the creation, and particularly rendered practicable in a unity of laws, government, and worſhip, by this univerſal equality eſtabliſhed among the various families ; which keeps the way open for the equal and gradual improvement of their common nature. This is the ſyſtem taught by revelation : it is a plan that reaſon readily acknowledges, and benevolence chearfully adopts ; it gives a grand, a flattering, and the only conſiſtent view of mankind, as having for its author the God of univerſal nature He, who once has entertained it, muſt deſpiſe the conjectures of philoſophy, and the paradoxes of infidelity. And ſurely it ſhould gain for that revelation which diſcovers it a fa-vourable, even an intereſted, hearing, equally from the politician and the philanthropiſt, as encouraging the nobleſt and warmeſt wiſhes that reſpect ſociety or man. \

All

All here is confiftent and analogical. In certain attributes and qualities, in the mental powers, all mankind agree. The feveral families or fuppofed races have various marks, connecting them with each other, and diftinguifhing them from the reft. The nations into which each each race is divided, with the common attributes of the race, have lefs apparent, yet ftill fufficient marks to diftinguifh them from others, and connect them together. Generally fpeaking, even inhabitants of provinces have a common run of manners, language, or features, perhaps of all taken together, to bind them in fome degree of union, and alfo diftinguifh them. After thefe, domeftic likeneffes take place, that have ftill more intimate common marks, yet allow of a fufficient variety to know a man from his brother.

Now, in the eye of true philofophy, the diftinguifhing attributes of the individual, an hair more or lefs of this or that colour, a particular feature predominant, have as certain a diftinct caufe in nature, as what makes the difference between the faireft European and moft jetty African. If, therefore, we can refolve the difcriminating attributes of individuals into the neceffary final caufe of focial intercourfe, why hefitate we in afcribing to the fame caufe the more obvious diftinctions of the greater families?

lies ? Or, why feek for caufes lefs confiftent, apparently lefs worthy of the Deity, to pamper vanity and pride, when this is full and fufficient to explain the fa&t ?

For the period when this diftin&tion took place, and the plan of reformation to which it looked, we are referred by Mofes to the confu- fion of Babel, " When the Moft High divided " to the nations their inheritance ; when he " feparated the fons of Adam ; when he fet " the bounds of the people according to the " number of the children of Ifrael :" a family, that, in the courfe of Providence, was feparated, and, when the fulnefs of time came, was em- ployed, to inftru&t the world in that common relation to their Creator and to each other, which had been entangled in error, disfigured by fable, and perverted by fi&tion: for this office the Jews were well calculated ; their turn for commerce made them wander and mix with, while their cuftoms kept them diftin&t from, other nations. They were a&tuated with zeal for the unity of the Deity, and fhewed a won- derful patience under perfecution.*

S E C T.

<hr />

* It is remarkable of Philo, the Jew Platonift, that though he gives no hint of his knowledge of Chriftianity, which alone explains and vindicates the Jewifh law, and points out its de- fign ; yet, with Chriftians and Platonifts, he fuppofeth the world to be the immediate work, and under the particular
government

SECT. II.

Objections to African Capacity, drawn from Form, confidered.

THE marks that diftinguifh the African, and give room to the tyrannic European (for I be-lieve the Afiatic mafter is content with the pre-eminence that power imparts) to claim the higheft

government of the Demiurgos, or word, and he affirms the feparation of the Jews to have had the gradual improvement of mankind in view.

In fpite of the obligations that the world in general owes to the Jews, refpecting theology and morality, yet fo fafhionable is it for every author, in imitation of Voltaire, to go out of his way to abufe them, that he who expreffes a regard for them expofes himfelf to contempt. But thofe who deny them the privileges of a particular difpenfation, in fo doing exalt them above all nations of antiquity. For they alone had penetra-tion to find out, and piety to worfhip, the univerfal Creator. The Roman twelve tables were a collection from all the Greek inftitutes; how contemptible are they compared with the de-calogue! That anciently the Jews were not the defpifed people which modern infidelity would fain reprefent them, appears clearly from the alliances formed by them, and the immunities and privileges granted them under the Perfians, Grecians, and Romans. The farcafm of Auguftus on them, may be accounted for from their being the only province that refufed to make him a God. The fneering of the Roman poets is, in the cafe of a conquered nation, but a poor proof of a matter of fact. But thefe cavillers have not reflected that the hiftory of the Jews, from which their abufe is drawn, con-fiders them wholly as objects of morality and religion, un-der the immediate government of the Lord Jehovah, not with other hiftories as a ftate rifing and falling in the fcale of opulence.

higheſt place, are, as I before obſerved, flat noſes, prominent chins, woolly hair, black ſkins; to which the curious anatomiſt adds ſkulls leſs capacious, calves of the legs leſs fleſhy, and elevated more towards the hams. Now, allowing all theſe, we want a link to connect them with inferiority. Leſs capacious ſkulls, ,indeed, will at once be deemed concluſive againſt us; but has the rule been applied, and is it found agreeable to obſervation in common life?

We know that climate, diet, and the various modes of life have great power over the features, form, and ſtature of man. Weſt Indian children, educated in England, improve not only in complexion, but in elegance of features: an alteration ariſing, perhaps, equally from change of climate, of diet, and of education.

opulence. Take the moſt virtuous people of this, or any ancient period, and meaſure their manners by the perfect law of God, and will they ſtand in a more amiable or praiſeworthy light than theſe deſpiſed out-caſts? Doth Jeremiah paint the depravity of his people in ſtronger lines than honeſt Latimer doth that of his age, though the period of reformation? Would Latimer ſoften his ſtile, were he to return among *us?* Farther, to be abuſed is a ſign of oppoſition and emulation rather than of inferiority. Why, among the various nations that inhabit the Britiſh iſles, is one alone abuſed by their wealthier neighbours, but becauſe it treads moſt cloſely at their heels? Had not the Jews made a diſtinguiſhed figure in the Roman Empire, the triumph that celebrated their conqueſt would have cloſed the account of them as a people.

tion. We fee fimilarity of features run through particular families. Shall we, therefore, be able to tell which carries the enfigns of genius; which bears the impreffion of wifdom, the proper foundation of power. On this fuppofition, hereditary indefeafible right in Kings would not be a fubject of ridicule, but of grave difcuffion. We need only to diftinguifh accurately the ftamp of royalty to put ourfelves under the beft poffible government. Were this allowed, we could no longer laugh at the Egyptians for pretending to be able to chufe out their God Apis from amidft herds of common oxen. We fee fets of national features independent of colour. We fee colour gradually verging from white to black, through every intermediate degree of tawny and copper. We fee genius fporting in various forms, tall in Newton, bulky in Hume, flender in Voltaire, diminutive and deformed in Pope. Where fhall we fix the claim of genius? how purfue it through all the diverfity of human form? Or, were we to attempt it, and infolently place ourfelves, or our tribe, in the higheft rank, would not HISTORY dafh the vain garland from our brow? Would it not tell us that arts, fciences, and the immediate capacity for them, are progreffive in their nature and objects, vifiting fometimes this region, fometimes another?

Again,

Again, of the fame fociety, of the fame family, fome men are fmooth, fome hairy, fome
tall, fome fhort, fome fair, fome brown. But
as thefe peculiarities are indifcriminately diftributed among individuals, otherwife equal, no
body thinks of applying a rule to meafure the
difference, or of afcribing to each ، its allotted
fhare of mental powers. Yet the moft minute
difference, a fhade more or lefs, of this or that
colour, muft have as diftin& a caufe to produce it, as what divides a man from a monkey.
And Mr. Hume, becaufe a tall bulky man, and
alfo a fubtile philofopher, might have denied
a capacity for metaphyfical fubtilty to all who
wanted thefe his great bodily attributes, as well
as fuppofe capacity and vigour of mind incompatible with a flat nofe, curling hair, and a black
fkin.

It is faid of negroes, that their brain is black-
ifh, and the glandula pinealis wholly black; a
remark of which the Cartefian, with his au-
dience-hall of perception, might make much.
It has not come within my notice; nor on the
principles of common fenfe can any thing be
inferred from it, unlefs anatomy had alfo determined that the jaundice affe&s not thefe parts,
as a proof that this blacknefs arifes not from
the colour of the fkin. But it is obferved that
their blood is of a dark red. This may be accounted

counted for from their poor falt diet, and their working naked in the fun; and this colour in the blood may contribute to thefe appearances in the brain, while running through the capillary veffels that are fpread over every vifible part of it.

The fkin takes its colour from a gelatinous fubftance, placed between the fcarf and the proper fkin: this fubftance approaches to jet black in proportion as the place of their nativity lies near the equator. In bad health, it equally, with the northern white, in the fame circumftances, changes into a fickly yellow. Is not colour a precarious foundation for genius, feeing, in one view, we may fuppofe it to reduce the parts of a fick white man, in another to increafe thofe of a fick negro, by bringing both nearer to a ratio of equality.

Perhaps an enquiry into the nature of freckles in fair complexioned people might throw fome light on the blacknefs of the African. The feat of their blacknefs and of freckles is the fame; and they appear to be allied in nature, being both, probably, a fecretion, and coagulation from the capillary veffels, brought about in particular circumftances by the miniftry of the weather and fun: for negroe children are born white, and the weather and fun caufe freckles.

When

When, therefore, we can account for the pre-
difpofing caufe of freckles in particular perfons,
we fhall know fomething of black fkins : for
a freckle may be defined a partial black fkin ;
a black fkin an univerfal freckle.   It may be
an help in the inquiry to remark, that a difpofition to be freckled and ftrong red curling
hair generally go together : as in this light, a
black colour may be deemed the effect of weather on a delicate fkin ; and freckles as a fimilar effect on fkins of a coarfer, though not the
coarfeft grain.   It would be curious to obferve,
among one's acquaintances, if their parts were
in the inverfe proportion of the finenefs of their
fkins ; or if a much freckled fkin, with its curling hair, as approaching to black, be a fign of
the owner's ftupidity or dulnefs.

In northern climates men have long hair, and
fheep have wool ; in fouthern climates fheep
have hair, and Africans woolly heads. In time
we may be able to account for both without
bringing genius into queftion.   The flat nofes
of negroes, in many cafes, may be accounted
for from the cuftom of being conftantly tied on
their mothers backs when infants, and nature
has prepared them for this, by fhortening the
cartilage of the nofe.   Sometimes they are procured, as an agreeable feature, by violence.
In general they are a national feature, like
the

the high cheek bones of the Scotch. Calves, fwelling little, and placed high, are frequent, but not univerfal, or even general, in the legs of negroes; nor feem they to prevail much more among them, efpecially among Creoles, than among the Creole whites, who are originally from Europe. Some negroes have legs, that in clumfinefs and lownefs of calves, may vie with an Irifh porter. The fame may be affirmed of the prominent chin: it is frequent, not general; a convex face is not a rare fight among them. If, therefore, an oblongated, or concave face be, as is fuppofed, connected with a fmall cerebellum, it is not their general attribute. On the other hand, I have amufed myfelf with obferving, that fome of the moft improved of my acquaintances may be remarked for prominence of chin.

Whether thefe diftinguifhing marks of negroes were, as we have fuppofed, fixed by the Author of nature, as part of that plan of particular fociety, and future reunion, that began with the race of man, whether caufed by climate, or given to enable them to bear the fervours of the torrid zone, or whether all thefe caufes have cooperated, while we conclude not on our fuperiority over them, is matter of innocent difputation. Of the laft-mentioned caufe it is certain, that though they work naked in the hotteft hours, their fkin never blifters, while

while vagabond white failors blifter wherever the fun reaches them ; and that they enjoy hot dry weather, while moifture and cold make them fhiver, and crouch down helplefs and fpent. On the whole, our obfervations are not of that length of time, and accuracy of manner, on which to build the fond opinion of northern fuperiority ; and reafon and revelation forbid the haughty thought. Suppofing the general fuperioity of Europe over the natives of the torrid zone, while we argue from thefe principles, how fhall we account for the Mexicans being lefs black, and more civilized within the equatorial girdle, than the Californians, inhabiting the region of genius, and white fkins ? or, according to the author of the obfervation, " how can improved fociety change an appa- " rent law of nature ?" Shall we fuppofe the equatorial circle to have been originally allotted to the black race, and that they have been expelled from all parts of it, except Africa ?

S E C T. III.

Objections to African Capacity, drawn from Anatomy, considered.

W E have gone through the several particulars, in which negroes visibly differ from white men, and find, that should they even mark a different race, they can in no respect determine their inferiority. We come now to consider, what may be indicated from diminutive skulls.

A gentleman, justly celebrated for his accuracy in the course of his anatomical researches, has discovered a surprizing difference between European and African skulls. This suggested to him the idea of drawing out a series of heads in this gradation ; European, African, monkey, dog. The difference between the two first, is indeed striking : the European, by the swelling out of the hinder part of the skull, supporting itself so as to shew the face almost perpendicular to the table on which it is placed; while the African, for want of such support, recedes from the perpendicular, and shews and obvious elongation of the lower jaw. The use that he has made of the discovery, has been the classing of the nations by their attributes, without taking genius into account. He rather throws it out but only as a conjecture, that negroes might have been the originals of mankind, he having observed, that

in

in all birds and beasts, the originals, whence the tame forts are derived, are black, and that every variation from them approaches more or lefs to white.

Other men, lefs modeft, have drawn from the obfervation, the conclufion of inferiority; it therefore will be neceffary to pay a particular attention to it, or rather to their deduction from it. And we fhall firft obferve, fuppofing this diftinction real, that it muft have fome benevolent and general purpofe; which purpofe we fhould fearch for, and follow out; which purpofe we know is not to feed pride, or indulge cruelty as thefe notions at prefent do. Matter of fact, or the real agency of nature, wherever difcovered, may be affumed for the foundation of our reafoning; nor fhould we vainly imagine that fhe ftands in need of our feigned apology, or wants to lie concealed behind the flimfey texture of our conjectures. We may be unacquainted with her workings, or with the particular purpofe that fhe means to carry on. But we need not therefore fear, left what comes from her hands be found fraught with abfurdity, or lead to principles deftructive of humanity, or derogatory to wifdom and goodnefs. Let then the fact be, that negroes are an inferior race; it is a conclufion, that hitherto has lain hid and unobferved, and while it leads only to an abufe of power in the fuperior race, it is

better

better concealed, than drawn out into notice. Perhaps Providence may keep it doubtful, till men be fo far improved, as not to make an ill ufe of the difcovery. I am fure, at prefent, the power, if it be a rig.t, is delegated to many improper perfons. In the mean time, while the fuperior race continues likely to abufe it, every ftep that leads to the eftablifhment of a point, the good purpofe of which lies hid, while the evil purpofe is ready at hand, fhould undergo and ftand the fevereft fcrutiny before it receives our approbation.

1. In this cafe it muft be eftablifhed as a maxim, that except in cafes of idiotifm, or accidental ill conformation, the rational powers are in proportion directly as the quantity of brains. And hence it will follow, that with the foregoing exceptions, we may, among Europeans, bring genius to actual admeafurement, and determine its degrees by the fize of the poffeffor's head, juft as an excifeman gauges a beer barrel. How much of thofe wranglings, that render us contemptible in the eyes of all Europe, fhould we fave in both houfes, if our competitors for power, inftead of wafting the nation's time in a war of words, fhould each fubmit his head to this fimple trial of its capacity ?

2. In

2. In the fecond place, this difference muſt
be univerſal, without a ſingle exception, unleſs
as above. For, as we have clearly proved,
there muſt always be a degree of excellence to
diſtinguiſh the loweſt of the ſuperior order,
from the higheſt of the inferior. And this, it
ſeems, in the caſe of the ſkull, is actually determined by the ſame gentleman againſt the
ſuppoſition; for there is in his poſſeſſion an
European ſkull of the ſame proportion as his
African. In confirmation, I may ſay, that I
know many inſtances, where the African excels
individual Europeans, in the exerciſe of the
reaſoning faculties.

3. That brains and reaſon are conſtantly in
a direct ratio, will be diſputed in determining
between the dog and monkey. I have heard
much of monkeys ; I have had opportunities of
obſerving them ; but nothing has led me to conclude, that they are equal, far leſs ſuperior, in
reaſoning and ſagacity, to that humble friend
of man, the faithful dog : certainly they are not
ſo teachable, nor ſo capable of being attached
by good offices, or gratitude. While on this
head, we may obſerve, that naturaliſts ſuppoſe
every various ſpecies of dog to come from the
ſhepherd's cur ; yet their ſhapes and qualities
differ more ſenſibly, than does the African from
the European.

4. Another

4. Another fact to be eftablifhed is, that the difcriminating fize of the African fkull, and confequent inferiority of reafoning, continue in the fixed civilized generations, and that, after no given period, do they approach to European capacity. But allowing the difference to be at firft real, I can, from obfervation, deny its continuance among Creole negroes.

Suppofing the diftinction to be found among the wilder tribes, we may well account for it in the following manner. Among favages, the powers of the mind are confined to few objects; and though their acutenefs refpecting them, in particular cafes, may exceed what can be imagined in polifhed life, yet certain it is, that we have few well attefted inftances of the capacity of favages, in attaining the various accomplifhments, and abftract notions, to be found in common among a civilized people. Their want of words in their native tongue, to exprefs, or communicate their ideas, would be a fufficient bar. And this may be one great caufe why, in North-America, the children of favages, after having been educated in the European manner, and taught to read and write, generally feize the firft opportunity of returning to the rude cuftoms of their fathers. Now we can perceive a gracious defign in what Providence denies, as well as in what it beftows. A man capable of varied knowledge, and verfatile exertion,

ertion, in a fituation where he had few or no objects to work on, would be unhappy in himfelf, and a curfe to all around him.* His defire, and power of exertion, are therefore confined within his opportunities and means of employment ; and we have only to try, and difcover the manner, in which nature has contrived to fit him for his rank. In doing this, we will confider the difference between the fkull and the reafon of an African, and thofe of an European, as an eftablifhed fact, from which we are to reafon.

Suppofe then an African, in his favage ftate, to have lefs brains, and in confequence lefs reafon, yet ftill a fufficiency for his fituation; the queftion then is, whether his head, his brains, and his reafon, would not expand in the fucceffive generations of civilized life. We know, that independent of the immediate organs of generation, the female, even in parts exactly fimilar to thofe in the male, is particularly adapted to the bearing, bringing, and fuckling of children. Now the way of life, and the degree of exercife, that the female has ufed from her birth, may either check, or favour her conftruction as a mother.

* What fad work would the authors of our prefent new fyftems in philofophy, religion, and government, make among the fimple Chiquefaws or Algonquins.

ther. In the favage ftate, where hunting is the chief means of fubfiftence, food muft be fcanty, and only to be procured by patience and exertion. Savages therefore, both male and female, will be found lean, dry, mufcular. And this condition will particularly affect the female, becaufe in almoft every favage tribe, fhe is confidered as a flave, intended to labour for, and ferve her hufband. Will not thefe circumftances, her fcanty diet, and violent exercife, affect the conformation of her body, and render the few children whom fhe brings forth, lean, flender, their heads fmaller, more elongated, the brain of a drier, lefs elegant texture, juft capable of that degree of intelligence which the favage ftate requires? And may we not afk, Is not this, in a certain degree, found to be the cafe of fuch women among us, as are habituated to hard labour ? Children of the loweft peafants, I believe, are as feldom found to take an high ftation in literature, as in elegance of form. The middle ranks of life, that fupply conveniencies to foften, not luxuries to drown nature, are moft favourable to elegance of form and acutenefs of underftanding. Fifhermen's wives, in the north of Scotland, labour more hardly than any other women in Britain ; and their neighbours look down with contempt on the ftupidity and ignorance found in the fifhing villages. Hence may be accounted for the care

K   taken

taken by the ancient Bramins to regulate the diet, exercife, and paffions of their pregnant women.

But fuppofe favages to be fo far civilized, as to be fixed in their habitations, to be well clothed, and properly fed ; fuppofe their wo-men treated with the regard that women ge-nerally receive in polifhed life, eafed of labour, employed only in regulating their family, or fupported in idlenefs, or amufement. Would not their bodies expand, and the fexual quali-ties attain an higher perfe&tion ? Would not the embryo be better nourifhed, the tender tex-ture of the brain be lefs injured, than when the pregnant woman ufed fcanty nourifhment, and violent exercife ? Would not the children be brought forth more plump ? Would not the brain, favoured in its growth, force the fkull to take its natural fpherical form, and according to our hypothefis, make the man more capable of improvement ? And, this, as far as my op-portunities of obfervation have reached, is the cafe of negroes who have been domeftic flaves for three or four generations in our colonies, or have been made free three or four generations. back.*

That

* The reafoning here ufed was fubmitted to the late celebrat-ed Dr. Hunter, who was pleafed to fay, That, as far as ana-tomy was concerned, he thought it fair and conclufive. The
fame

That there is any effential difference between the European and African mental powers,
as far as my experience has gone, I pofitively
deny. That there may be an accidental or cir-
cumftantial difference, I can eafily fuppofe, and,
fhould it be true, think I can fee the reafon of
it, as above explained. And this opinion is farther ftrengthened by remarking, that, as far as
the hiftory of polifhed fociety goes back, both
Afiatic and European women have, from the
firft, been generally indulged, and accuftomed to
a domeftic fedentary life, favourable to the
bearing and fuckling of fuch children as might
be capable of advancement in the departments
of reafon, and in all that varied intelligence
which polifhed life calls forth and ftands in need
of. We have indeed one exception, and it is
favourable to our conclufion. The Spartan

fame gentleman, in his courfe of lectures at the Royal Aca-
demy, when fhewing the gradation of fkulls, a difcovery
which he candidly gave to its right Author, humanely obferved, that he drew no conclufion from the difference in them
refpecting African inferiority. Several perfons, who had poffeffed the beft opportunities of obferving the capacity of Africans, had affured him, that there was no difference to be feen,
but what could be traced to their depreffed condition, and that
there were inftances where African ability had fhewn itfelf in
fpite of all the difadvantages under which it laboured. He
underftood, that the very doubt whether they might not be
an inferior race, operated againft the humane treatment of
them ; and God forbid, faid he, that any vague conjecture of
mine fhould be ufed to confirm the prejudice.—Such was the
modefty of true genius.

K.2   women

women were accuftomed to a poor diet, and violent exercife, even to contending and wreft-ling with men.   And it is well known, that a-mong the polifhed Greeks, the Spartans were a nation of favages : their language, like that of other favages, broken, yet expreffive ; their knowledge confined to war, but to the part of a mere foldier ; for they were once fo abfolutely without a citizen fit to command their army, that they were obliged to employ a lame Athe-nian fidler as a general. Nay, fo late as the Perfian war, they were forced to fend to the Athenians to get inftructed how to attack a bar-ricado, made of baggage implements.   Nor a-mong the numerous artifts and philofophers that Greece produced, are any celebrated as Spar-tans by birth.   For, if Lycurgus is to be rec-koned an exception, we muft fay, that he form-ed the Spartan difcipline, but was not himfelf formed by it.   If one or two individuals of that ftate are to be ranked amonged the philofo-phers, for uttering a few abrupt fentences, there is not a chief among the American favages but has an equal, perhaps a fuperior, title to the ftation.

S E C T. IV.

Objections to African Capacity, drawn from Observation, considered.

THE ingenious author of a late History of Ja-maica, has treated this subject at considerable length, and appears to have formed, from his own observation, the same opinion as Hume's, of negroes being a distinct race. To suppose them only a distinct race, will not immediately affect our arguments for their humane treat-ment and mental improvement ; but the confe-quences usually drawn from it shock humanity, and check every hope of their advancement : for, if allowed to be a *distinct* race, Euro-pean pride immediately concludes them an *in-ferior* race, and then it follows, of course, that nature formed them to be slaves to their supe-riors. And the master having established these premises generally, and complimented himself with a place among the superior beings, fairly concludes himself loosed from all obligations, but those of interest, in his conduct towards them. A horse and a bull, are animals each of a different species; but the superiority has not been established between them, nor the inferior brought into bondage by the lordly master. For argu-ment's fake, suppose negroes of a different and even

of

of an inferior race, ftill we know they are capable of forming, and actually have formed, free independent focieties; and, though they have not yet attained the refinements and luxuries of Europe, yet have they fhewn no fmall ingenuity in compacting themfelves together, and made no mean progrefs in many of the arts of life. And to help to compofe, and be a member of a free ftate, is more honourable, and gives greater fcope to the mental powers, than to be the moft polifhed flave in America or Europe. Still being fuch, are they to be dragged away from a country adapted to their conftitutions, from plenty of nutritious food, to which they have been accuftomed from infancy,* to work as flaves, hungry, naked, torn with ftripes, in a diftant, unfavourable clime, for the avarice and lufts of, perhaps, fome of the moft worthlefs perfons of the pretendedly fuperior families, with whom they had neither acquaintance or connection? Suppofe different races, and that they vary in point of excellence; yet, in what chapter of nature's law is it declared, that one quarter of the globe fhall breed flaves for the reft? Where fhall we find a charter conferring authority on the one, and

---

* Left this fhould feem to contradict the reafoning drawn from their original favage ftate, it is neceffary to obferve that the flaves, as brought from Africa, differ greatly, in refpect of ability, according as the nation from which they have been kidnapped has advanced more or lefs in focial life.

afcertaining

afcertaining the fubmiffion of the other? Are no conditions annexed, no rights referved, which, when violated, the fubjected race can plead before their common Lord? Such a ftate cannot be imagined as exifting under the government of God: it is blafphemy againft his benevolence even to fuppofe it. The inanimate and brute creation was fitted for and fubmitted to man's dominion; but man himfelf was left independent of every perfonal claim in his fellows. And nothing but an implied voluntary furrender of his independency to fociety, for the benefits of law can control or leffen his claim. But North-American or Weft-Indian flavery implies no furrender, fuppofes no fubmiffion, but to neceffity and force.

Had nature intended negroes for flavery, fhe would have endowed them with many qualities which they now want. Their food would have needed no preparation, their bodies no covering; they would have been born without any fentiment for liberty; and, poffeffing a patience not to be provoked, would have been incapable of refentment or oppofition; that high treafon againft the divine right of European dominion. A horfe or a cow, when abufed, beaten, or ftarved, will try to get out of the reach of the lafh, and make no fcruple of attempting the neareft inclofure to get at pafture. But we

have

have not heard of their withdrawing themfelves
from the fervice of an hard mafter, nor of aveng-
ing with his blood the cruelty of his treatment.

To fuppofe different, efpecially fuperior and
inferior races, fuppofes different rules of conduct, and a different line of duty neceffary to
be prefcribed for them.   But where do we find
traces of this difference in the prefent cafe?
Vice never appeared in Africa in a more barbarous and fhocking garb, than fhe is feen every
day in the moft polifhed parts of Europe.   Europe has not fhewn greater elevation of fentiment than has fhone through the gloom of A-
frica.   We can fee caufe why the nations, into which for the purpofes of fociety mankind
has been divided, fhould have characteriftic
marks of complexion and features, (and almoft
the whole of the prefent fubject of difcuffion
may be refolved into thefe) to tie, by the refem-
blance, fellow-citizens more clofely and affectionately together.   And, be it remarked, that
thefe figns are mere arbitrary impreffions, that
neither give nor take away animal or rational
powers; but, in their effect, are confined to
the purpofe for which they appear to have
been impreffed, the binding of tribes and families together.   Farther, climate, mode of living,
and accidental prevalence of particular cuftoms,
will account for many national characteriftics.

But

But the foul is a fimple fubftance, not to be diftinguifhed by fquat or tall, black, brown, or fair. Hence all the difference that can take place in it is a greater or lefs degree of energy, a more or lefs complete correfpondence of action, with the circumftances in which the agent is placed. In fhort, we can have no idea of intellect, but as acting with infinite power and perfect propriety in the Deity, and with various degrees of limited power and propriety, in the feveral orders of intelligent created beings; fo that there is nothing to diftinguifh thefe feveral created orders, but more or lefs power; and nothing to hinder us from fuppofing the poffible gradual advancement of the lower into the higher ranks of created beings. But we cannot, in like manner, fpeak of the change of a bull into an horfe, or of a fwine into an elephant. The annihilation of the one is included in the tranfmutation into the other, becaufe in it that is loft which conftituted the fpecific difference.

We can plainly fee the propriety of different purfuits, and different degrees of exertion of the reafoning energetic powers in the feveral individuals that compofe a community, for carrying on the various purpofes of fociety. But there is not, therefore, a neceffity to have recourfe to different fpecies of fouls, as if the peafant had one fort, the mechanic a fecond, the man of

K 5 learning

learning a third; yet whatever concludes for the propriety of races differing in point of excellence, will conclude alfo for a difference in thefe. And we fee, in contradiction to all fuch reveries, that communities flourifh in proportion as the lefs of any other difference takes place, than that in which fociety naturally difpofeth of its members for their mutual or joint benefit. The foul is verfatile, and being fimple in itfelf takes its manner and tincture from the objects around it; it univerfally appears to be fitted only for that character in which it is to act: but that this is not an indelible character appears plainly in every page of the hiftory of mankind. Look into our books of travels, and, in perfons no ways remarkable for genius or invention, admire the almoft incredible efforts and productions of neceffity. How often has the fhepherd fhone out as a ftatefman, and the peafant triumphed as a general? Can we fuppofe greater difference between the African and European, than, for example, between the keeper of fheep, and the Governor of men; between leading an herd of gregarious animals out to pafture, and directing the complicated genius and bent of that various creature man, either to counteract or attain the purpofes of fociety: yet the only difference between them lies in the direction given to the mental faculties.

Thus

Thus far we have oppofed opinion with argument, and, excepting a remark of which we fhall take notice, we may leave all that the author above-mentioned has advanced of the inferiority of negroes, to be contrafted with the inftances given by himfelf of their energy, abilities, and fentiment, and to be compared with the inftances of ftupidity to be found in the moft polifhed nations. For, as we have proved, if we eftablifh the notion of different races, we muft ftill draw a line between the higheft of the one, and the loweft of that next above it. Particularly, we may fay of his example, Francis Williams the negroe poet and mathematician, that though his verfes bear no great marks of genius, yet, there have been bred at the fame univerfity an hundred white mafters of arts, and many doctors, who could not improve them; and, therefore, his particular fuccefs in the fields of fcience cannot operate againft the natural abilities of thofe of his colour, till it be proved, that every white man bred there has outftripped him. But allowance is to be made for his being a folitary effay, and the poffibility of a wrong choice having been made in him. Childifh fprightlinefs, for which it feems he was fingled out for the trial, is not always, nor indeed often, a faithful promifer of manly parts; too frequently it withers without fruit, like the early bloffoms of the fpring. Other gentlemen of

Jamaica

Jamaica fpeak highly of his abilities, and of the favour they procured for him.

The remark in this author referred to, is that Mulattoes cannot propagate their kind with each other, or, at leaft, that their children are few and fhort-lived. Now it fhould be obferved that Mulattoe girls, during the flower of their age, are univerfally facrificed to the luft of white men; in fome inftances, to that of their own fathers. In our towns, the fale of their firft commerce with the other fex, at an unripe age, is an article of trade for their mothers and elder fifters; nay, it is not an uncommon thing for their miftreffes, chafte matrons, to hire them out, and take an account of their gains; or, if they be free, they hire their fervice and their perfons, to fome one of the numerous band of bachelors. In this commerce they often contract difeafes, and generally continue in it till grown haggard and worn out. Thus few Mulattoes marry in their own rank, and fewer in a ftate of health favourable to population. But where the above circumftances take not place, Mulattoe marriages are extremely prolific, in every inftance within my knowledge; and I can recollect more than fix fuch families where there is a numerous healthy offspring, and no doubt to be entertained of their legitimacy. As intellect is the peculiar attribute of man, and is a fimple fubftance, it is incumbent

on

on thofe who maintain a difference in races and natural abilities, to tell us how the fuperior in-tellects of a white perfon, and the inferior in-tellects of a negroe unite, and become a *tertium quid*, in their Mulattoe offspring. Is nature at the expence of forming feparate and different conditioned intellects for all the variety of cafts between complete white and black in our feveral colonies ? *

S E C T.

* In the above difcuffion we have affumed the exiftence of intellect as confidently, as if modern philofophy had not afferted man to be organized matter. The affertion, though unac-companied by conviction, is fuch a check to every afpiring thought, that hardly, fince I heard of the difcovery, have I been able to reconcile one to myfelf; nor can I endure an opi-nion which would rob me of a comfort that fmoothed every ill of life, and encouraged me to look up to futurity for a recom-pence, which my Heart told me was referved for the humble and benevolent. It is true, that the abettors of it profefs to believe, with Chriftians, man's future reftoration. But if man be a mere combination of atoms, when that combination is broken by death, the Being formed by it is annihilated. A reunion of the fame particles will conftitute a new Being, having no moral refpect to what happened to the firft, neither ftained with its blame, nor inheriting its merit. Indeed imagination can-not combine together the idea of merit and matter, becaufe all the motions or actions (if we could ufe the term) of matter muft be neceffary and mechanical. The villain who *murders*, the Samaritan who *faves*, a man, deferve equal applaufe. Volition, or the act of thinking, brings into exiftence fome new motion or form. But can we imagine fuch a power lodged with matter, which muft itfelf receive from without every particular impreffion, every new direction ?

Suppofe matter capable of thinking, and the man to have every nerve employed in purfuing a certain train of reafoning;

from

S E C T. V.

African Capacity vindicated from Experience.

HAVING fhewn how little can be rationally concluded againſt the capacity of negroes, from their

from what energy, what attribute of matter fhall we deduce the power of ſtopping in the full career of inquiry, and taking at once an oppoſite path ? If thinking be the effect of organization, we can ſuppoſe no principle, no power lodged in the man to controul or direct it. It muſt proceed mechanically, till it be ſtopt mechanically. The man who reflects on what paſſeth in his mind, will perceive a difference between that inward act which weighs circumſtances, and that which determines him on action. But deliberation is incompatible with every notion of matter, becauſe it muſt ever be forcibly carried away by the predominant weight or power. To deliberate on, or balance circumſtances, muſt ſuppoſe ſome principle endowed with the power of election ; but of this, matter, as matter, is incapable.

We cannot take into account what the Deity poſſibly can do in the plenitude of power. Wherever his works lie open to inquiry, we obſerve, that he invariably proceeds according to the original nature of the ſubject. Fire never freezes, froſt never warms. But if the Deity give to matter the power of thinking, he ſuperadds an attribute analogous to no other quality of matter within our knowledge. He can give to a bull the form and attributes of an horſe. But is not the bull annihilated, and a new animal formed in his ſtead ? In like manner, to give to matter the ability of thinking, it muſt be changed into ſpirit, becauſe the attribute of thinking is incompatible with matter, even as the diſtinguiſhing qualities of an horſe cannot co-exiſt with thoſe of a bull.

The

their equatorial settlement, flat nose, woolly head, projecting chin, high calves, and black skin, we come to fact. Now we know, that house negroes, who are generally Creoles, and are conversant with their white masters, have all the address, intrigue, and cunning of family servants in Europe. In their masters they can mark the ridiculous point, the improper conduct, and often give these superior beings that advice, which they have not wisdom enough to follow; often manage their foibles, and mould them to their own interest. If, according to the Marchioness

---

The weight of a material being is the weight of its parts taken together, and may be divided into as many lesser weights as there are component parts; its extent is a number of extents, in proportion to the number of its extended parts; and thus it holds of every quality, with which we are acquainted, except this new discovered attribute, no new quality being produced by the composition. We can affirm nothing of the whole that may not be affirmed in part of every particle. But we cannot thus divide volition into parts, or scatter it among the several limbs or organs, nor even share it between the cerebrum and cerebellum. It is one simple uncompounded act.

If it be necessary to suppose a principle distinct from matter, to give form, motion, order, and design to things, may we not also suppose, that such creatures as men, who feel these active powers within themselves to a certain degree, may also be endowed with a portion of that spirit, which alone can begin and impress motion on inert matter.

Merit has been ascribed to him who neglected the body to have leisure to improve the mind; but on this scheme it is intirely absurd. He who cares for the body cares for the whole man. A glutton is not an object of ridicule, but of sober praise; he is employed in perfecting his ability to think.

chiomefs d'Ancre, favouritifm and influence be marks of fuperiority, many Weft-Indian families muft allow a prefemnce to the Africans.

Negroes are capable of learning any thing that requires attention and correctnefs of manner. They have powers of defcription and mimickry that would not have difgraced the talents of our modern Ariftophanes. The diftillation of rum, the tempering of the cane juice for fugar, which may be confidered as nice chemical operations, are univerfally committed to them. They become good mechanics ; they ufe the fquare and compafs, and eafily become mafters of whatever bufinefs they are put to. They have a particular turn for mufic, and often attain a confiderable proficiency in it without the advantage of a mafter. Negroe fick nurfes acquire a furprizing fkill in the cure of ordinary difeafes, and often conquer diforders that have baffled an hoft of regulars. Nor want they emulation, in whatever their obfervation can reach. Hence our black beaus, black belles, black gamefters, black keepers, black quacks, black conjurers, and all that variety of character, which ftrikes in their mafters, or promifes to add to their own dignity or intereft. But what can we expect them to attempt in the higher departments of reafon ? Their flavifh employments and condition ; their being abandoned to the caprice of any mafter ; the fubjection in which it is thought neceffary

to

to keep them all; thefe things deprefs their minds
and fubdue whatever is manly, fpirited, inge-
nuous, independent, among them. And thefe
are weights fufficient to crufh a firft-rate human genius.

Had it been the lot of a paradoxical Hume,
or of a benevolent Kaims, to have cultivated the
fugar-cane, under a planter, in one of our old.
iflands ; the firft probably would have tried to
have eked out his fcanty pittance of two pounds
of flour or grain per week, by taking up the
profeffion of a John Crowman, or conjurer; and
doubtlefs would have got many a flogging for
playing tricks with, and impofing on the cre-
dulity of his fellows, to cheat them of their
allowance. The turn of the other to works
of tafte might have expreffed itfelf in learning
to blow a rude fort of mufic from his noftril,
through a hollowed piece of ftick ; or, if bleffed
with an indulgent mafter, he. might have
learned to play by ear a few minuets, and fiddle
a few country dances, to enable the family and
neighbours to pafs an evening cheerfully together.

The truth is, a depth of cunning that enables them to over-reach, conceal, deceive, is
the only province of the mind left for them,
as flaves, to occupy. And this they cultivate,
and

and enjoy the fruits of, to a furprizing degree.
I have, as a magiftrate, heard examinations and
defences of culprits, that for quibbling, fub-
terfuges, and fubtilty, would have done credit
to the abilities of an attorney, moft notorioufly
converfant in the villainous tricks of his profeffion. Their command of countenance is fo
perfeċt, as not to give the leaft clue for difcovering the truth; nor can they be caught trip-
ping in a ftory. Nothing in the turn or degree of
their mental faculties, diftinguifhes them from
Europeans, though fome difference muft appear, if they were of a different or an inferior
race.

I had a young fellow, who was a notorious
gambler, idler, liar, and man of pleafure; yet
fo well did he lay his fchemes, fo plaufibly did
he on all occafions account for his time and con-
duċt, that I, who could not punifh unlefs I could
convince the culprit that I had undoubted proof
of his guilt, was hardly ever able to find an
opportunity of correċting him. This lad, when
he came a boy from Africa, fhewed marks of
fentiment, and of a training above the common
run of negroes. But flavery, even in the
mildeft degree, and his accompanying with
flaves, gave him fo worthlefs, diffipated a turn,
that I was obliged to fend him out of the family, and have him taught a trade in hopes of
his

his reformation. By this he infenfibly acquired a little application, and has fince attached him-felf to a wife. His father, he fays, was a man of property, had a large houfhold, and many wives. He was kidnapped.

There is another lad, who could ftand without flinching to be cut in pieces by the whip, and not utter a groan. As whipping was a triumph, inftead of a punifhment to him, I was obliged to overlook the moft notorious faults, or affect generoufly to pardon them, rather than pretend to correct them. Yet this proceeds not from infenfibility of pain, for if bleeding be prefcribed for him when fick, he cries like a child, and fhrinks from the operation. About twelve years ago he was caught in a fault, that by the cuftom of the colony would have juftified his mafter in carrying his punifhment to any degree, fhort of extremity. Pains were taken to fet the enormity of it before him, and he was freely pardoned, and his fellows were ftrictly forbidden ever to upbraid him with it. Since that time he has behaved remarkably well and truft-worthy, and fhewn a very uncommon attachment to the family. A third boy, who is fenfible as a little lord of every affront offered to his dignity, could ftand with the fullen air of a ftoic to receive the fevereft correction.

In

In truth, in ſpite of the diſadvantages under which they labour, individuals, on particular occaſions, have ſhewn an elevation of ſentiment that would have done honour to a Spartan. The Spectator, No. 215, has celebrated a rude inſtance in two negroes, in the iſland of St. Chriſtopher, which on inquiry I find to be true. I will confirm this by the relation of a deed, that happened within theſe thirty years, for which I have no name. As I had my information from a friend of the maſter's, in the maſter's preſence, who acknowledged it to be genuine, the truth of it is indiſputable. The only liberty I have taken with it, has been to give words to the ſentiment that inſpired it.

Quaſhi was brought up in the family with his maſter, as his play-fellow, from his childhood. Being a lad of towardly parts, he roſe to be driver, or black overſeer, under his maſter, when the plantation fell to him by ſucceſſion. He retained for his maſter the tenderneſs that he had felt in childhood for his playmate; and the reſpect with which the relation of maſter inſpired him, was ſoftened by the affection which the remembrance of their boyiſh intimacy kept a live in his breaſt. He had no ſeparate intereſt of his own, and in his maſter's abſence redoubled his diligence, that his affairs might receive no injury from it. In ſhort, here

was

was the moft delicate, yet moft ftrong, and feemingly indiffoluble tie, that could bind mafter and flave together.

Though the mafter had judgment to know when he was well ferved, and policy to reward good behaviour, he was inexorable when a fault was committed; and when there was but an apparent caufe of fufpicion, he was too apt to let prejudice ufurp the place of proof. Quafhi could not exculpate himfelf to his fatisfaction, for fomething done contrary to the difcipline of the plantation, and was threatened with the ignominious punifhment of the cart-whip; and he knew his mafter too well, to doubt of the performance of his promife.

A negroe, who has grown up to manhood, without undergoing a folemn cart-whipping, as fome by good chance will, efpecially if diftinguifhed by any accomplifhment among his fellows, takes pride in what he calls the fmoothnefs of his fkin, its being unrazed by the whip; and he would be at more pains, and ufe more diligence to efcape fuch a cart-whipping, than many of our lower fort would ufe to fhun the gallows. It is not uncommon for a fober good negroe to ftab himfelf mortally, becaufe fome boy-overfeer has flogged him, for what he reckoned a trifle, or for his caprice, or threatened him with a flogging, when he thought he did

not

not deferve it. Quafhi dreaded this mortal wound to his honour, and flipt away unnoticed, with a view to avoid it.

It is ufual for flaves, who expect to be punifh-ed for their own fault, or their mafter's caprice, to go to fome friend of their mafter's, and beg him to carry them home, and mediate for them. This is found to be fo ufeful, that humane maf-ters are glad of the pretence of fuch mediation, and will fecretly procure it to avoid the neceffity of punifhing for trifles; it otherwife not being prudent to pafs over without correction, a fault once taken notice of; while by this method, an appearance of authority and difcipline is kept up, without the feverity of it. Quafhi there-fore withdrew, refolved to fhelter himfelf, and fave the gloffy honours of his fkin, under fa-vour of this cuftom, till he had an opportunity of applying to an advocate. He lurked among his mafter's negroe huts, and his fellow flaves had too much honour, and too great a regard for him, to betray to their mafter the place of his retreat. Indeed, it is hardly poffible in any cafe, to get one flave to inform againft another, fo much more honour have they than Europeans of low condition.

The following day a feaft was kept, on ac-count of his mafter's nephew then coming of age; amidft the good humour of which, Quafhi

hoped

hoped to fucceed in his application; but before
he could execute his defign, perhaps juft as he
was fetting out to go and folicit this mediation,
his mafter, while walking about his fields, fell
in with him. Quafhi, on difcovering him, ran
off, and the mafter, who is a robuft man, purfued him. A ftone, or a clod, tripped Quafhi
up, juft as the other reached out his hand to
feize him. They fell together, and wreftled
for the maftery, for Quafhi alfo was a ftout
man, and the elevation of his mind added vigour to his arm. At laft, after a fevere ftruggle,
in which each had been feveral times uppermoft,
Quafhi got firmly feated on his mafter's breaft,
now panting and out of breath, and with his
weight, his thighs, and one hand, fecured him
motionlefs. He then drew out a fharp knife,
and while the other lay in dreadful expectation,
helplefs, and fhrinking into himfelf, he thus addreffed him. . " Mafter, I was bred up with you
" from a child; I was your play-mate when a
".boy; I have loved you as myfelf; your in-
" tereft has been my ftudy; I am innocent of
" the caufe of your fufpicion; had I been
" guilty, my attachment to you might have
" pleaded for me. Yet you have condemned
" me to a punifhment, of which I muft ever
" have borne the difgraceful marks; thus only
" can I avoid them." With thefe words, he
drew the knife with all his ftrength acrofs his
own

own throat, and fell down dead without a groan, on his mafter, bathing him in his blood.

Had this man been properly educated; had he been taught his importance as a member of fociety; had he been accuftomed to weigh his claim to, and enjoy the poffeffion of the un-alienable rights of humanity; can any man fuppofe him incapable of making a progrefs in the knowledge of religion, in the refearches of reafon, or the works of art? Or can it be af-firmed, that a man, who amidft the difadvan-tages, and gloom of flavery, had attained a re-finement of fentiment, to which language can-not give a name, which leaves the bulk of po-lifhed fociety far behind, could want abilities to acquire arts and fciences, which we too often find coupled with a fawning, a mean, a flavifh fpirit? Others may, I will not believe it.

This is a truly mournful inftance of a noble-nefs and grandeur of mind in a negroe. The following, though allied to diftrefs, is of a lefs awful nature, but will fhew, that all the nobler qualities of the heart are not monopolized by the white race.

Jofeph Rachel was a black trader in Barba-does; he dealt chiefly in the retail way, and was fo fair and complaifant in bufinefs, that in a

town

town filled with little peddling shops, his doors were thronged with cuftomers. I have often dealt with him, and found him remarkably honeft and obliging. If any one knew not where to procure an article, Jofeph would be at pains to fearch it out, to fupply him, without making an advantage of it. In fhort, his character was fo fair, his manners fo generous, that the beft peo-ple fhewed him a regard, which they often deny men of their own colour, becaufe not bleffed with like goodnefs of heart.

In 1756 a fire happened, which burned down great part of the town, and ruined many of the inhabitants. Jofeph luckily lived in a quarter that efcaped the deftruction, and expreffed his thankfulnefs, by foftening the diftreffes of his neighbours. Among thofe who had loft their all by this heavy misfortune, was a man to whofe family Jofeph, in the early part of life, owed fome obligations. This man, by too great hof-pitality, an excefs common enough in the Weft-Indies, had involved his affairs, before the fire happened, and his eftate lying in houfes, that event intirely ruined him; he efcaping with only the clothes on his back. Amidft the cries of mifery and want, which excited Jofeph's compaf-fion, this man's unfortunate fituation claimed particular notice. The generous, the open tem-per of the fufferer, the obligations that Jofeph had to his family, were fpecial and powerful

L motives

motives for acting towards him the friendly
part.

Joseph held his bond for fixty pounds sterling.
" Unfortunate man," says he, " this shall
" never come against thee.   Would heaven thou
" could settle all thy other matters as eafily!
" But how am I fure that I shall keep in this
" mind: may not the love of gain, efpecially,
" when, by length of time, thy misfortune has
" become familiar to me, return with too strong
" a current, and bear down my fellow-feeling
" before it?   But for this I have a remedy.
" Never shalt thou apply for the affiftance of
" any friend against my avarice." He got up,
ordered a current account that the man had with
him, to a confiderable amount, to be drawn out,
and in a whim, that might have called up a fmile
on the face of charity, filled his pipe, fat down
again, twisted the bond, and lighted his pipe
with it.   While the account was drawing out,
he continued fmoking, in a ftate of mind that a
monarch might envy.   When finished, he went
in fearch of his friend, with the account difcharged, and the mutilated bond in his hand.
On meeting with him, he prefented the papers
to him with this addrefs.   " Sir, I am fenfibly
" affected with your misfortunes; the obligati-
" ons that I have received from your family, give
" me a relation to every branch of it.   I know
" that your inability to fatisfy for what you owe,

                                   " gives

" gives you more uneafinefs than the lofs of
" your own fubftance. That you may not be
" anxious on my account in particular, accept
" of this difcharge, and the remains of your
" bond. I am over-paid in the fatisfaction that
" I feel, from having done my duty. I beg
" you to confider this only as a token of the
" happinefs that you will impart to me, when-
" ever you put it in my power to do you a good
" office." One may eafily guefs at the man's
feelings, on being thus generoufly treated, and
how much his mind muft have been ftrengthened
to bear up againft his misfortunes. I knew him
a few years after this; he had got a fmall poft
in one of the forts, and preferved a decent appearance.

But his hofpitable turn continued even after
he had loft the means of indulging it. He has
often invited five or fix acquaintances, or
ftrangers, to fpend the evening when he has not
had even a candle to light up before them.
Whenever his fervant faw him come home thus
attended, and heard him call away, as in his
better days, his refource was to run over to
Jofeph, and inform him that fuch and fuch gentlemen were to fup with his mafter. Immediately the fpermaceti candle, and punch, and
wine of the beft quality were on the table, as
if by magic; and foon after Jofeph's fervants
appeared, bringing in a neat fupper, and wait-

ing

ing on the company. All this was done without a profpe&t of return, purely to indulge his gratitude, and fupport his friend's credit. And will any man pretend to look down with contempt on one capable of fuch generofity, becaufe the colour of his fkin is black?

Some readers, perhaps, may give Jofeph more credit for the following ftory. A colonel ————, a moft penurious mifer, ufed to call frequently at Jofeph's fhop, on pretence of cheapening cocoa: he was always fure to carry away as much for a tafte as his pocket would hold, but never bought any. Jofeph, at firft, was at a lofs what to do. He knew, that, being a negro, his evidence would not be taken in court, even for the value of a penny againft a white man. But the colonel continuing his depredations, he was loth to fee his cocoa diminifh daily before him without any thing in return for it. He therefore hired a white man for clerk, and ordered him to weigh out a bag of cocoa, and keep it particularly under his own care, to fupply the colonel with taftings whenever he fhould call. The colonel foon emptied the bag, and then Jofeph delivered in his account. The colonel ftormed, fwore, and threatened till out of breath, when Jofeph took the opportunity of informing his honour of the fteps he had taken. His avarice now alarmed him with the expences of a law-fuit: and fuggefted

that

that being fo fairly taken in, there was nothing to be done, in prudence, but to pay the money peaceably. By this innocent ftratagem Jofeph got rid of the colonel's tafting vifits.

I fhall only give one more inftance in favour of the negroes ; though a volume might eafily be filled. A lieutenant of a regiment in garrifon. at St. Chriftopher's died, and left his fon an orphan. A particular family had promifed him, on his death-bed, to take care of his boy ; but he was wholly abandoned, and forced to keep among the negroe children, and live on fuch. fcraps as he could find. In this ftate, he caught that loathfome difeafe the yaws, which. became a new reafon for giving him up to his fate. In this ulcerated condition, Babay, a poor negrefs, found him, took him into her hut, got him cured, and maintained him till he was able to work for himfelf. The firft money that he earned went to purchafe her fieedom. He took her home to his houfe, and, as long as fhe lived afterwards, which might be upwards of forty years, treated her with the moft refpectful kindnefs. He gave her a moft expenfive burial, and had a funeral fermon preached over her. As that fermon was delivered before people acquainted with her character, and mentioned fuch circumftances as I wifh here to remark, I fhall give an extract of what was addreffed to the flaves that attended, relating

relating to her. " This good woman was like
" many of you, a flave; and, as fuch, la-
" boured under every difadvantage which you
" can plead for not doing your duty; yet, in
" this fituation, fhe fhewed, in her conduct,
" the nobleft fruit of religion, charity. A
" helplefs child, left an orphan, in a ftrange
" country, far from any relation or even ac-
" quaintance to his family, abandoned by thofe
" who undertook to rear him, from her alone
" could raife pity, or engage attention. When
" left, by all of his own rank and colour, to
" perifh in a loathfome difeafe, though fon to
" a fervant of the public, with whom every
" true lover of his country fhould have fympa-
" thized, fhe, alone, lodged him, nurfed him
" carefully, got him cured, and put him in a
" way to provide for himfelf. This inftance
" of generofity, found in one of her condition,
" is a proof that noble and difinterefted actions
" are not, as many think, confined to advan-
" tages of birth or education; for fhe had
" nothing to direct her but God's grace working
" on a tractable heart: and this benevolent
" temper fhewed itfelf in every part of her
" behaviour through life, and was accompanied
" in her with a true fenfe of religion. She
" was well acquainted with what fhe ought to
" know and believe; and always fpoke of
" religion with an earneftnefs, and ferioufnefs,
" and knowledge, which I wifh were more
                                        " general

" general than I have found it among thofe
" who efteem themfelves her betters. Here
" then is a fhining example of goodnefs, on
" your own level, for your imitation." *

* The following thoughts have been communicated lately
to the author by a humane intelligent fea officer, who, in his
command on foreign ftations, did not think he went out of
his line by pleading and promoting the caufe of humanity.
They are particularly pertinent in this place to prove Africans
proper objects of improvement and police.

" I have talked, I have written ; I have often blufhed for
" the unnatural tyranny exercifed in our Weft Indian Ifles ;
" where Proteftants even exceed Papifts in barbarity to the
" unfortunate flaves that have become their purchafed pro-
" perty. Particularly, I have, in the warmeft manner, re-
" commended their imitation of the Roman Catholics in
" beftowing baptifm on their flaves, inforcing my argument
" from this confideration :" "-You acknowledge the Chriftian
" path, in which you walk, to lead to a happy future ftate ;
" how can you then, as men or Chriftians, refufe that to your
" flaves, which you believe will intitle them to falvation ?"
" I cannot boaft of the impreffions that thefe arguments made
" in our Weftern Archipelago. But, finding the planters in
" the colonies adjoining to Spanifh fettlements, complaining
" that their flaves were daily deferting from them, I thought I
" had found an argument to urge intirely in their own way :"
" Your flaves defert to the Spaniards, becaufe they grant them
" greater privileges than you do, and make Chriftians of them.
" Ufe you the fame methods, and they will not think of
" leaving you."

" The negroes along the fea-coaft of Africa (particularly
" among the French) are well-informed, eafy, kind, generous,
" and have a better fenfe of right and wrong than any other
" people I have ever vifited. I was thrown among them in a
" ftate of wretchednefs and ficknefs, with feventy-feven dying
" men, being abandoned by our own people, who refufed me
" affiftance and medicines. I caft myfelf on the charity of
" favages,

" favages, and received more inftances of compaffion and
" goodnefs from them than from all the Chriftians I have eŮer
" known. From this exemplary benignity in this people,
" who are inhabitants about Cape Verd, may be collected the
" probability of introducing freedom and Chriftianity among
" them."

" On the fouthern continent of Africa the natives are well
" informed, well clad, dwell in fuperb houfes, abound in
" cattle and other poffeffions. Some Portuguefe are fettled
" among them, but, I believe, they draw their knowledge,
" merchandize, and grandeur from their communication with
" Mozambique, Arabia, and Egypt. The places I chiefly
" refer to, are Paulo Loando and St. Philip de Buengala."

CHAP.

C H A P. V.

Plan for the Improvement and Converfion
of African Slaves.

I HAVE now gone through the feveral prelimi-
nary articles that refpect flaves in our fuglar colonies. I have defcribed their condition at prefent.
I have fhewn that there would be good policy and
much profit, both to the ftate and the mafter,
in advancing it ; that this advancement muft go
hand in hand with their inftruction in religion ;
and, again, that inftruction is neceffary to make
them good and ufeful fubjects. I have vindicated for them the natural equality and common
origin of mankind. I have claimed, as their
due, the attention of government. I have endeavoured to intereft humanity, policy, and religion in their favour. It only remains to
point out the method in which thefe fhould co-
perate for their advantage. That which I am
now to offer, I propofe not as the beft poffible,
but as the moft practicable method, having refpect to the felfifhnefs and prejudices of the age.
Were government and people once well awakened to their own intereft, and heartily inclined,

L 5

fomething much more promifing might be
ftruck out. The chief advantages of the following plan is, that it may be fet on foot by government, without depending on the caprice of
individuals, or affecting their intereft ; that it
will be gradual in its operation, and therefore
more likely to accommodate itfelf to the ordinary courfe of human affairs. At the worft, it
adds only one more to the many Utopian fchemes
that volunteer reformers produce for the benefit
of the heedlefs public. Should it ever be found
as impracticable in itfelf, as it is in refpect of
me, it may lead fome more happy man to a
fcheme both practicable and fuccefsful. In the
mean time it may contribute to foften their prefent treatment ; and it will be a teftimony of
the author's affection to the caufe of humanity,
religion, and his country. The event muft be
left to Providence. It will be adapted to the
ftate of a particular colony ; but may eafily be
accommodated to others. I fhall only premife,
that the feveral hints occafionally given in the
courfe of the work, and what has been fuggefted in the cafe of particular plantations,
chap. III. fect. V. is offered to every other
owner of flaves, as far as circumftances will
permit.

S E C T.

S E C T. I.

Eſtabliſhment of Clergy, and their Duty among Slaves.

THE iſland of St. Chriſtopher's, of which we particularly treat, is divided into nine pariſhes, and is, at preſent, ſupplied by five miniſters ; the emoluments of two pariſhes being barely ſufficient for the decent ſupport of a family, without ſuppoſing any proviſion made for a widow and children. But, to carry on our plan of reformation among ſlaves ; nay, indeed for the due ſupport of an eſtabliſhed religion among the white inhabitants, it would be neceſſary that each pariſh ſhould have its own incumbent. This would give the proportion of one miniſter to about 3000 inhabitants ; but it would require the proviſion allotted for their maintenance to be increaſed. Of this proviſion I ſhall not at preſent treat ; though, whenever it becomes an object of police, it will be eaſy to propoſe a fund for their decent maintenance without any ſenſible new expence to government or people, and chiefly by changing the mode of certain preſent impoſts. In the proportion here ſuggeſted, many pariſhes, eſpecially in Jamaica, would require to be divided ; but the miniſters could eaſily and profitably
fitably

fitably for the colony be provided for there by allotments of unappropriated funds. *

I would propofe alfo a fchool to be eftablifhed in each parifh ; the fchool-mafter to be under the minifter's direftion, and to affift in inftructing and bringing forward the young children. A houfe, the place of parifh clerk, and fome other fmall appointment, with the benefit of fcholars, would always procure decent men for the office. †

Suppofe

* Barbadoes contains eleven parifhes, each with its minifter; the town parifh has alfo a fixed curate. In Antigua there are fix parifhes, and fix minifters. In.Montferrat there are four parifhes, and two minifters. In Nevis five parifhes, and three minifters. In Grenada there are ufually two minifters without appointments ; it is the fame in Dominica. In St. Vincent's there are two minifters, and very fmall appointments. In Tortola there is no fixed minifter. In Anguilla the minifter has been long dumb for want of a maintenance. In Jamaica there are nineteen parifhes, fome of them as large as the whole Leward Infland government, and fome of them without church or minifter.

† Indeed a very fmall proportion of thofe immenfe fums that are thrown away under pretence of educating their children in England, would procure men properly qualified to fettle in thefe fchools in the iflands, which would not only fave to the parents much needlefs expence, but alfo preferve the morals of the youth, and train them up to be ufeful to themfelves and families. A young Weft-Indian, configned to a fugar-factor to be educated at a diftance from his father, foon begins to know no other relationfhip between him and his parent, than that of banker. He makes expenfive connections, acquires habits of diffipation,

Suppofe then a proper number of fober, pious minifters fettled in the colonies, each in his own cure, and employed in the duties of his function, fupported by government, and encouraged by good men. Let the minifter, every Sunday, perform the ufual·morning fervice to his white parifhioners, and fuch fenfible negroes as can attend; in the afternoon let the fervice be adapted to the negroes. Inftead of a common fermon, let him explain to them, in courfe, a chapter of the New Teftament, making them intimately acquainted with the miffion and hiftory of our Saviour, and our relation to him, as the immediate Creator, Head, and Redeemer of the world. Let the clergyman frequently give a fhort expofition of the apoftle's creed, in eafy terms, and explain the ten commandments in words adapted to their capacity.

Let the minifters jointly compofe forms of devotion, fome to be ufed in private by the negroes, others for their field morning and evening prayers, and others, more comprehenfive,

---

diffipation, is never made to feel his own weight, and feldom learns to turn out ufefully in life. Where parents have not the vanity or are not in circumftances to fend them to England, but content themfelves with giving them an ufeful education near them, Weft-Indian children fhew that they want neither capacity nor application.

to

to be ufed by the whole gang on Sundays, in the plantation. Let them be drawn up fhort, fimple, inftructive, expreffive, of their relation to God, to a Saviour, to fociety, and of the refpect that a candidate for heaven owes to himfelf. Indeed it would be found a great advantage in carrying on the. work, if the forms were compofed to ferve in all the colonies generally. Mafters fhould be exhorted to fend, at convenient times, their moft fenfible flaves to the minifter, to be inftructed in thefe forms, that they may teach the reft, and take the lead in the plantation evening and morning devotions. . If the mafter, manager, or overfeer, were conftantly to lead their Sunday plantation devotions, it would have an excellent effect. Negroes, who are well treated and in fpirits, fing at work. A few eafy fingle ftanzas might be collected or compofed, to be ufed inftead of their common fongs. In every thing drawn up for them, the expreffion fhould be. fimple, and the meaning obvious.   .   : .

Let the minifter vifit the plantations in rotation, at convenient times, to inquire into the behaviour and improvement of the flaves, to commend, reprove, admonifh, and pray with them. To give him refpect and influence, let all be obliged to appear before him decently clothed.   .

Let

Let him pay a particular attention to children; that while their minds are tender, before their difpofitions be foured by the impofitions of flavery, they may make fome progrefs in the knowledge of their duty. As they may be better fpared from plantation work than the reft, they may attend on the minifter on particular week days for inftruction.

In common cafes, no culprit fhould be punifhed by the matter, who can find a fenfible fober negroe to be furety for his good behaviour: but both furety and culprit fhould be frequently admonifhed by the minifter of the nature of the engagement; and this practice would give him many opportunities of imprinting on their minds the obligations of virtue, the claims of fociety, the difference between right and wrong. In fhort, one circumftance that has happened among themfelves, properly difcuffed before them and imprinted on their minds, will have a better and more lafting effect than a thoufand difcourfes on general good and evil.

Wherever there is room for fhewing mercy, it fhould be done at the minifter's interceffion, that he may be confidered as a mediator between the flave on one fide, and the mafter and the law on the other. He fhould never appear in any other light among them than that of their inftructor

inftructor and benefactor, praying with them, interceding for them, or doing fome good office to them; that their efteem for his perfon, and gratitude for his kindnefs, may ftand to them in place of a law, may produce in them a love for his doctrine, and be a pledge of their good be-haviour to the community. One caufe of the author's little fuccefs among his own flaves was, doubtlefs, the neceffity of mixing the autho-rity of the mafter in domeftic matters, with the exhortations of the teacher; and the fuperior fuc-cefs of the Moravians may be accounted for, from their being feen by their fcholars, only in the benevolent light of inftructors.

The minifters fhould have monthly meetings at each other's houfes, to which well-difpofed gentlemen of the neighbourhood fhould be oc-cafionally invited : at thefe they might talk over their difficulties, their fuccefies, their plans. Every meafure fhould be carefully difcuffed be-fore carried into execution ; the plan of inftruc-tion fhould be uniform; the prayers, precepts, hymns, fhould all fpeak one language. And we might hope that the minifters, relieved by a de-cent provifion from worldly care, countenanced by government, refpected by good men, and en-couraged by each other in this good work, would foon find pleafure in it, and fee it profper in their hands.

But

But fome greater care fhould be taken in the choice of perfons defigned for this labour, and of candidates fent over from the colonies for ordination, than has been hitherto ufual. It is now growing into a cuftom, in the Weft-Indies, for men that have diffipated their patrimony, to flee to the church as their laft refuge from poverty, often with very flender pretenfions refpecting education, and lefs refpecting decency of character. Yet, if any diftinction were proper, the colonifts, even fetting afide this plan of the converfion of their flaves, by reafon of their ufual careleffnefs and diffipation, require a fuperior attention to the character of their paftors. Perhaps the fitteft perfons that could be fent out would be difcreet curates from England, accuftomed to teaching, whofe hopes of preferment are fmall, to whom thefe fettlements would be a defirable advancement. The Society for Propagating the Gofpel might have a committee to examine, felect, and recommend them to the feveral governors.

S E C T.

SECT. II.

General Improvement of Slaves.

I HAVE vindicated the natural capacity of African flaves, have laid before the reader their prefent condition, have proved that to advance them in religion and focial life would profit both the public and their mafters, and have propofed a plan for their inftruction. We may now make this inference refpecting the original defign of this work. Were the yoke of flavery made to fit more eafy on their necks; were they taught to think more juftly of themfelves, more moderately of their mafters; did their condition admit of the enjoyment of the common conveniencies of life; were thefe extended and fecured to them; were their families and offspring to be confidered as their own, not wantonly to be torn from them at the caprice, or to pay for the extravagance of their tyrant; then would they be found capable of arts that are ufeful in fociety here, and of extending their own views to futurity. Then, when they had become fenfible of their relation to God, would his religion, which we wifh to introduce, have a fair chance among them; they would efteem themfelves more worthy of it, more nearly connected with it, more ftrictly obliged to inquire into its doctrines,

and

and conform their lives to its laws. Then, in refpect of intellect, would they be found equal to the people of any country.

French flaves enjoy a great advantage for the admiffion of religion over Englifh flaves, in the familiarity that French manners permit them to live in with white people : an advantage that is increafed by the prefence of their owners, who generally live and converfe with them, fuperintend and partake with them in their labours, inftead of fubmitting them to hirelings ; many of whom, in fullen filence, think of nothing but of extorting labour out of them, at the expence of health, life, and every human feeling ; and are, indeed, often obliged to do this to keep up the remittances, and preferve their places. The above-mentioned circumftances in the French iflands conceal the diftance between mafter and flave, make the diftinction eafier to the latter, and, by exciting equally their affection and ambition, pave the way for introducing among them the cuftoms and religion of their mafters.

The difficulties which the French had to conquer in their firft attempts to convert flaves cannot now be afcertained. But, long fince, cuftom and time have made the work eafy to them. Religion, as they teach it, places particular merit in the work of converfion, which

is

is a fpur to their piety. The Creole flaves
know no other religion than Chriftianity. The
new African flaves are gradually abforbed into
the mafs. With the firft rudiments of a new language, they draw in the precepts of a religion
that mixes itfelf with every mode of common
life ; as foreigners are faid to learn Englifh, by
the oaths and imprecations with which our
tongue abounds. Thus they acquire the religion gradually, with the cuftoms of their new
country, while attention and curiofity are ftrong
on them, before they have been put to hard or
difagreeable labour, to difguft them with the
manners and worfhip of their mafters. It muft
be owned, indeed, that the Romifh mode of
worfhip, confifting of pomp and ceremony, is
better calculated to ftrike, *at firft fight*, the imagination of ignorant people, than our fimple
ritual. A remark, that may explain the attention which a very oppofite fect, the Moravians,
pay to forms in managing favages, and the
ftrefs that they lay on the defcription of our
Saviour's fufferings and crucifixion ; as if it was
neceffary for improving the mind, to make religion a mechanic exercife, and draw piety as
an object of fenfe.

On the other hand, till the minds of our
flaves be more enlightened, till their fituation be
made more eafy, till they have a refuge againft
the effects of the caprice, ignorance, cruelty,
                                        poverty

poverty of their mafters, till they think themfelves intitled to the protection of fociety, we
cannot expect them to take their proper rank
in the ftate, nor to make any confiderable progrefs in religious knowledge. At prefent they
know and feel nothing of fociety, but the hardfhips and punifhments that it cruelly and capri-
cioufly inflicts; they lie far beyond its care, and
out of the circle of its comforts. And I believe
it will be found that Chriftianity has feldom
made any great progrefs, except where fociety
was in an advanced ftate. Nor has it fupported itfelf, but in the polifhed parts of Europe and America. And how, rationally fpeaking, can it happen otherwife? A conformity
with revealed religion fuppofeth a conqueft over
the felfifh paffions; and unlefs we be firft accuftomed to facrifice, in a certain degree, thefe
paffions, for the advantages of fociety, which
come home to our immediate feelings, we fhall
hardly be willing to facrifice them for the hopes
of religion. Indeed the benevolence or charity,
which is the corner-ftone of Chriftianity, is
evidently a refinement on juftice, which is the
bond of fociety. But, can we refine on a law
that doth not exift? As religion muft be built
on a foundation of law; fo, in refpect of practice, it may be called the perfection of fociety:
it brings futurity into the aid of law, and gives
a moral fanction to the edicts of authority.
Could it find admittance among favages, it
· would

would of neceffity polifh them, and introduce
fociety among them. Modern philofophers
and politicians, even while exerting their influence to undermine its foundations, give religion this teftimony : " Though too vulgar a
" ftudy for a fine fpirit, and its precepts too
" mean for his free fentiments, yet religion is
" an excellent inftrument in the magiftrates
" hands to make the mob harmlefs, fober, in-
" duftrious, honeft, and obedient †."

And conformably to this reafoning we find,
it was in the cities, where fociety had improved
the underftanding, that the apoftles and their
fellow-labourers chiefly made converts to Chriftianity. A Pagan or country clown, and an
heathen or infidel, foon became equivalent
terms. Different, indeed, is the cafe now,
when our fine wits, (who, had they lived in the
early

† There is at laft, indeed, one exception in the newly erected ftates of America : they have almoft generally declared
againft an eftablifhed religion as a neceffary part of their conftitutions ; the fuccefs cannot for fome time be known.

The good effects of religion, in improving fociety, is nobly
teftified in the fuccefs of the Moravians among the favages of
Greenland : by gradually introducing Chriftianity and induftry together, of felfifh precipitate favages, they have made a
band of provident, fober, ufeful, fympathifing brethren. Their
progrefs there is the triumph of religion over ignorant un-
affifted reafon. Yet our flaves are much more civilized than
thefe originally were; but liberty, nature's inheritance to man,
more than compenfated to them the difference.

early ages of Chriſtianity, merely for the credit of their parts, would have been moſt ortho-
dox) are aſhamed of the religion of their fathers;
and, rather than profeſs any religion in common with mankind, will maintain the ſillieſt
paradox, the moſt degrading dogma. I wiſh,
indeed, we could ſay, that good manners, and
obedience to the laws, were not generally ſent
away with what they affect to call bigotry :.
ſo indiſſolubly bound together are the characters of a good citizen and pious man.

In general the faculties of the mind muſt be
expanded to a certain degree, before religion
will take root, or flouriſh among a people;
and a certain proportion of civil liberty is neceſſary, on which to found that expanſion of
the mind, which moral or religious liberty
requires.* By this aſſertion I exclude not particular inſtances; but ſuch neither form nor
confute general rules. To bring this home to the
caſe of our ſlaves: the great obſtacle to government

* When Moſes led the children of Iſrael out of Egypt, he
was under the neceſſity of training them up to be an independent people, by multiplied forms and ſtrict diſcipline, for the
ſpace of forty years. And it is apparent, from their behaviour
during this long period, that ſlavery had ſo thoroughly debaſed their minds, as to have rendered them incapable of the
exertions neceſſary for their ſettlement in the promiſed land,
till all thoſe who had grown up as ſlaves in Egypt, had fallen
in the wilderneſs, and laws and regulations worthy of a free
people had taken place among them. This is a caſe full in
point, and may ſuggeſt hints worthy of the legiſlature.

ment in bringing about this point, ſetting aſide its own careleſſneſs in ſuch things, is the alteration that it would at firſt make in private property. This it is true we have in chap. 2, ſeĉt. 3. ſhewn to be more in appearance than in faĉt. But ſuch are our prejudices, that any law to improve the condition of our ſlaves, or to inſtruĉt them in the principles of religion, would be too apt to be conſidered as an encroachment on their maſters property, and an hinderance of their profit.

Still allowing this prejudice its full operation, ſomething conſiderable might be done by parliament, by colony legiſlatures, by willing conſcientious maſters. Expedients would offer themſelves, methods might be diſcovered, to advance the condition, and promote the religious intereſts of ſlaves, and ſave alſo, or even improve, their labour to their maſters, and the ſtate. Nay, the intereſt of the ſtate would ultimately be advanced by every indulgence extended to them. On the other hand, little can any other individuals attempt, and leſs can they effeĉt, except to pray that the minds of our governors may be enlightened to ſee the honour and advantage of this undertaking. We come now to ſuggeſt ſuch an advancement of their condition, as may lay the foundation of that improvement, in morality and religion, which is the objeĉt of this work.

S E C T.

S E C T. III.

Privileges granted, and Police extended to Slaves.

WE have obferved, that flaves are hardly in any inftance confidered as objects of police, being abandoned to the management, or rather caprice, of their feveral mafters. Nor doth law take notice of them, but to enforce power, which, without fuch affiftance, too frequently lays reafon and humanity bleeding at its feet. Our laws, indeed, as far as they refpect flaves, are only licenced modes of exercifing tyranny on them ; for they are not made parties to them, though their lives and feelings be concluded by them. As well may directions for angling be faid to be laws made for dumb fifh, as our colony regulations for whipping, hanging, crucifying, burning negroes, be called laws made for flaves. To make them objects of civil government muft therefore be an effential part of every plan of improvement that refpects flaves ; fo that while obnoxious to the *penalties* of the law, they may be intitled to its *fecurity* ; and while law leaves them under the *management* of a mafter, it may protect them from his *barbarity.*

A judge fhould therefore be appointed to determine difputes of confequence between mafter

.M   and

and flave, as in the French colonies.* The power of the mafter fhould be reftrained within certain limits. He fhould not be fuffered to maim, beat, or bruife wretches with a ftick. To flit ears and nofes, to break legs, or caftrate, † fhould make a man infamous for ever, and, equally with the greater excommunication, incapacitate him from being evidence, or taking inheritances; and much more fhould fuch cruelties fhut the door againft him from fitting in an affembly, or council, as a legiflator. The fentiment of a gentleman, a native of St. Chriftopher's, pleafed me on this fubject. " Were a white fervant to behave to me as my " flaves often do, I fhould be provoked to beat " him moft unmercifully. But how can I ftrike " a wretch, who dare not ftrike again, who has " no law to which he may apply for fatisfaction " for my excefs, who has none but myfelf to " look up to for protection againft my vio- " lence?" What pity is it, fince fociety interpofes not, that fuch fentiments fhould be uncommon?

---

* If it be objected that the appointment of a judge would encourage flaves to be running conftantly to him with complaints, and annihilate the mafter's juft authority; the example of Athens formerly, and France now, may be adduced in proof, that no fuch effects neceffarily follow.

† The laft inftance of this enormity was, I believe, perpetrated by an Englifh furgeon in Granada.

If

If any flave has been flagrantly ill treated by a
mafter, the mafter fhould have a mark of infamy,
as above, fixed on him, and the flave fhould be
made free without price: or, if he be unacquainted with any trade by which he can earn
his bread, he fhould be fold for the benefit of
the public, at an eafy rate, to fome confiderate
man. To make a flave free, who cannot earn,
an honeft living, would be inhuman and impolitic. It is letting loofe on fociety a thief in
defpair.

The marriages of flaves fhould be put under fome better regulation than at prefent;
when a man may have what wives he pleafeth,
and either of them may break the yoke at their
caprice. Nothing would more humanize flaves,
and improve their condition, than their acquiring a property in their wives and families, and
having a reftraint laid on the promifcuous intercourfe of the fexes. Marriage, or a family,
is the embryo of fociety; it contains the principles, and feeds of every focial virtue. The
care of a family would make them confiderate,
fober, frugal, induftrious. An ambition to promote the condition of their children, would
fharpen and improve their talents. They would
avoid every fault, or meannefs, that might hurt
the intereft or credit of fuch dear relatives;
even as in polifhed fociety, a man who is married,

ried, is generrally found a more ufeful and truft-worthy citizen, than he who continues fingle. *

The minimum of a negroe's allowance for clothes and provifions fhould be fettled by law. Slaves fhould be allowed at leaft Saturday afternoon, as in Jamaica, for their own work, and to wafh their clothes. Sunday fhould be wholly their own, for the purpofes of inftruction,

---

* I admire that policy of the Athenians, which allowed no unmarried man to hold any place in the magiftracy, army, or navy. They did not depend on *his* fidelity to diftribute juftice, or defend the ftate, who had not given to the public a wife and children, as fureties of his good behaviour.

I mean not here to cenfure men, who, like Newton, pre-ferve themfelves chafte and fingle, the more clofely to apply to the ftudy of nature, or the intricacies of fcience. Neither the common good, nor moral rectitude, require the matter to be fo ftrictly urged. Let the poet court his mufe, or the phi-lofopher hold dalliance with nature, or fport in the fields of li-terature ; we will not permit the cares of a family to interrupt his refearches, or difturb his amufement. Matrimony claims only thofe in each fex, who find themfelves drawn irrefiftibly to the other, and wifhes only to fanctify their commerce. No plea can be ufed for the celibacy of thofe who keep not them-felves chafte. There is a forry felfifhnefs in their ftealing all that they value in the ftate, and leaving the cares to others. For they muft acknowledge, that in every community a cer-tain proportion muft marry ; and if it be a burden, why are they exempt ? Not but if this were the place to prove it, marriage might be fhewn to be, generally fpeaking, the only rational foundation for focial happinefs, and the ftate the God of nature appointed for man.

tion, and reft from labour. Their little properties fhould be fecured to them; their families
fhould not be torn from them. All plantation flaves, as at prefent is the cuftom in Antigua, fhould be confidered as fixed to the free-
hold, that they may not be fold, or carried
away wantonly at pleafure. It would then be
the next natural ftep, to tafk them as propofed in note, page 110, and fuffer them, by
their extra labour, to work out their freedom;
ftill taking care to keep as many of them attached to the foil, as might be wanted to carry
on the ftaple manufactures of the colonies as
day labourers.

Thefe regulations would lay a foundation
for that far diftant view which we take of this
fubject; the time when liberty fhall claim every
exiled African for her own child. Their being
connected with the foil, will draw after it certain perfonal rights, and all the claims of a family. Having once tafks affigned them, wages
will follow, and the bargain become mutual and
equal between the employer and employed *.
If, on account of ill behaviour, or any particular caufe, a mafter be under the neceffity of

M 3   parting

* One infeparable confequence of the communication of the
leaft degree of liberty or privilege to flaves, would be a defire
to be baptized, and to be confidered as Chriftians; for this
they think fecures the poffeffion of it to them. And much
good might be done towards their inftruction, by making a
proper advantage of this bias to the religion of their matters.

parting with a plantation flave, or banifhing him, let it be done with the approbation of the judge; and let the tranfaction, with the reafon affigned, be regiftered. In like manner fhould every decree given by the judge be regiftered.

To improve their minds, the flaves fhould be accuftomed to determine, as jurors, on the behaviour of each other. This would infenfibly lead them to diftinguifh between vice and virtue. What rendered the Grecian and Roman mobs (for their affemblies were no better) fo fuperior to the nations around them, but the privilege of being conftituted judges both of public mea-fures and private caufes, and, as fuch, of being daily improved by the public orations of their lawyers and ftatefmen? The frequent attendance on our courts of law, and as jurymen in the trial of caufes, which moft people in our little colonies are obliged to give, except they bribe off their appearance, imparts a precifion and readinefs in thinking to the colonifts, that one fhall in vain look for in the mother country in the fame rank, on the fame fubjects. Yet they are often very unpolifhed beings, when Europe firft fends them out among us.

Mafters fhould be encouraged to grant free-dom to fuch flaves as fhewed merit, and pro-mifed to make good ufe of it; but they fhould
be

be reſtrained from turning off ſlaves when become incapable of labour, as is often done, under pretence of giving them freedom. All colony laws, enaſted on the narrow principle of perſonal diſtinſtion, to prevent or fetter manu-miſſion, ſhould be annulled; ſuch as thoſe of Barbadoes and Granada, that fix a heavy fine to the public on the maſter who frees a ſlave. All mulattoes ſhould be ſent out free, trained to ſome trade or buſineſs, at the age of thirty years. Children of mulattoe girls ſhould be free from their birth, or from the commencement of their mother's freedom. Intendants ſhould be appointed to ſee them put in time to ſuch trade or buſineſs, as may beſt agree with their inclination, and the demands of the colony. This ſhould be done at the expence of their fathers, and a ſufficient ſum might be depoſited in the hands of the church-wardens, ſoon after their birth, to anſwer the purpoſe; the intendant keeping the church-wardens to their duty. This caſe ſuppoſes the mother to be free. If a man has a mulattoe born to him by another man's negreſs, he ſhould pay to her owner eight pounds ſterling, as ſoon as the child is weaned. It ſhould then be conſidered as the maſter's child, to be ſent out free as above. If the parent or maſter has negleſted to inſtruſt them in ſome uſeful calling, he ſhould be fined in an annuity equal to their main-tenance,

By

By thefe means, the number of free citizens would infenfibly increafe in the colonies, and add to their fecurity and ftrength. A new rank of citizens, placed between the black and white races, would be eftablifhed. They would naturally attach themfelves to the white race, as the more honourable relation, and fo become a barrier againft the defigns of the black. Nay, were the law extended to free every fenfible negrefs (and they are generally do-meftics, and fempftreffes) who fhould bring a mulattoe child by her mafter, or any man worth as much as would repay her value to her mafter, I fee no ill confequences that could follow from the regulation. At leaft, if it checked this improper commerce between mafter and flave, it would promote legal, and more honourable connections with their own equals. Still thieves, and vagabond beggars, fhould be excepted from every privilege, and be kept, or reduced to flavery, whenever difcovered ; and if this were the law, under certain reftrictions, even in Britain, much wealth and happinefs would redound from it.

On thefe outlines of fociety, viz. the indif-foluble tie of marriage, the claims of a family, the allowance of property, the afcertaining the hours and time of labour, or allotting it by tafk ; the fixing the minimum of maintenance and

and clothing ; the adjudging them to the foil ;
the making them arbiters of each other's conduct ; the affigning them a protector or judge,
to preferve their little privileges, and fecure
them againft cruelty ; in fhort, on the vindicating for them the common rights of humanity, would we erect a plan, that fhould
look forward to their gradual improvement,
and extend, by flow but fure fteps, to the full
participation of every focial privilege. Thus
fecured from injury, thus partaking in the fruits
of their own labour, they might be refigned to
the care of the paftors that we have propofed
for them, to be built up in holinefs, and the
fear of God, and taught to look forward with
refignation and hope, to a ftate where every
hardfhip, every inequality, infeparable from the
lot of humanity, fhall be intirely removed, and
fully compenfated.

CONCLUSION.

I HAVE now laid before the public what
I fuppofed might bear the light ; not all I have
thought, not all I have written on the fubject.
In many points fentiment has ftruggled with the
felfifhnefs of the age, and been obliged to fupprefs many a generous wifh : the feelings of
benevolence have been forced to give way to the
fuggeftions of narrow policy ; and even a fenfe

of

of the public intereſt has been made to yield to private prejudice. Yet if our ſlaves were once accuſtomed to taſte only a *few* of the ſweets of ſociety, a *little* of the ſecurity of being judged by known laws, they would double their application to procure the comforts and conveniencies of life ; and, with their additional property, would naturally riſe in their rank in ſociety. Many, eſpecially if our plan of working them by taſk were to take place, would, in time, be able to purchaſe their own freedom. Their demands for manufaCtures would increaſe, and extend our trade ; they would acquire a love for the country and government that ſhewed this attention to them. The labour of ſuch as became free might, for ſome time, be regulated on the ſame plan as that of labourers in England. Under the awe of, or rather aſſiſted by, a few regular troops, they might ſafely be truſted with arms for the defence of themſelves, their families, their own, and patron's property. Then would the colonies enjoy a ſecurity from foreign attacks that no proteCtion from Europe can afford them.

The minds of theſe, our fellow-creatures, that are now drowned in ignorance, being thus opened and improved, the pale of reaſon would be enlarged ; Chriſtianity would receive new ſtrength ; liberty new ſubjeCts. The ſlave
trade,

trade, in its prefent form the reproach of Britain, and threatening to hatten its downfal, might be made to take a new fhape, and become ultimately a bleffing to thoufands of wretches, who, left in their native country, would have dragged out a lite of miferable ignorance ; unknowing of the hand that framed them ; unconfcious of the reafon of which they were' made capable ; and heedlefs of the happinefs laid up in ftore for them.*

Thus, by a timely interpofition of the legiflature, and a judicious attention to circumftances, might Britain acquire a confiderable acceffion of ftrength, have its trade and taxes improved, and a large number of ufeful fellowfubjects, that are now funk in mifery and bondage, made happy here, and capable of happinefs hereafter. And thefe are confiderations that, furely, are fufficiently powerful to unite the worldling and politician, with the pious faint and fincere Chriftian, to carry on the fcheme as one man, fince each would find his feparate account in it. Honour, profit, piety, all

* This is on the fuppofition that the flave trade could be conducted without that violence and injuitice to individuals, and enormous lofs of lives in the paffage from Africa, and, during the feafoning in the colonies, that now accompanies it. For the greateft benefit that can poffibly happen to a few cannot juftify us for endeavouring it by murder, by violence, bad air, and famine, in making the experiment. They muft offer themfelves willingly for the voyage, and be better accommodated and treated during the courfe of it.

all join in the important requeſt; all ſolicit to have their claims to this benefit conſidered.

And what glory would it be to Britain, what an objeĉt of emulation, to enlarge the benevolent plan of France and Spain, for improving the condition of their ſlaves; and to open a way for the admiſſion of reaſon, religion, liberty, and law among creatures of our kind, at preſent deprived of every advantage, of every privilege, which, as partakers of our common nature, they are capable of and entitled to!

We have notoriouſly and continually thruſt ourſelves into the quarrels of others, and been laviſh of our blood and treaſure for the protection of ſtrangers and the advancement of ungrateful rivals, whoſe good-will, even in appearance, we could retain no longer than while our aſſiſtance was uſeful to them. But theſe miſerable wretches live only, *can* live only, for our profit, for our luxury. They have no proteĉtor, no refuge to flee to; and every penny laid out for their advantage would return with tenfold uſury to us. And ſhall we, from year to year, continue to ſpend our riches and ſtrength, in raiſing up thankleſs rival ſtates, and deny theſe unhappy beings a poor pittance of their own labour to make them a farther advantage and glory to us? Forbid it, honour; forbid it, juſtice; forbid it, prudence;

forbid

forbid it, humanity. What is here propofed may, poffibly, on trial, be found ineffectual, though I have good ground to think it would not. But, furely, were the feelings of humanity, the refearches of knowledge, and the obfervations of experience, collected in the confultation, they could not fail in producing fome plan capable of anfwering the wifh of reafon, religion, liberty ; capable of fecuring thefe bleffings to Britain and her children. Reafon will not be backward in a work that is to produce her advancement ; Liberty will think no conceffion great that is to extend her empire ; Piety will not reckon that expence exceffive that has the purchafe of fouls in view. Even felfifh Intereft will open her ears to the fuggeftions of accumulation. Slow methodical difcretion muft prefide over, and guide the gradually opening fcene. What unwearied application have the premiums offered for the difcovery of the longitude given rife to ? And what object more worthy of public encouragement than this, which propofes to recover to reafon, to utility, and happinefs, a multitude of human creatures drowned in ignorance and wretchednefs ?

Though what is here written, if deemed worthy of notice, will certainly expofe the author to much abufe from men, whofe wifhes and intereft, as they imagine them to tend, are

N   oppofed

oppofed to all reformation; yet, is he not fenfible of having had any thing finifter, felfifh,
or cenforious in view; nor can he, in any refpect, be particularly benefited if the improvement were to take effect? He has intended no
flight or injury to individuals, or to any condition or community of men, feparated from
their oppofition to the unalienable rights of human nature and the dictates of benevolence and
religion. His confolation is, that a fimple love
of truth, and a fincere defire to do good, alone
excited him to the attempt, and that many
pious and learned perfons thought it worthy
the attention of the public. And after ferioufly
reviewing the whole, he fees no objection to be
offered beforehand, either againft the practica-
bility, or expence of the plan, except the manners and prejudices of the age. On the contrary, there are confiderations to encourage both
individuals and government to make the attempt; arguments of ftrength, not only to be
drawn from topics of humanity, liberty, religion, but alfo of fafety, conveniency, pofitive
intereft, and profit, both public and private.

Doubtlefs, in a fubject like this, where we
muft be fatisfied with general accounts, probable conjectures, and analogical reafoning,
a perfon inclined to take the other fide may
felect many things to be objected to, many
to be contradicted. But, till fuch a man can,
                                        fimply

fimply and generally fpeaking, vindicate on the fcore of religion, morality, or even policy, the conduct, or rather negligence of government, with refpect to the fugar colonies; till he can prove, that the diet, the clothing, the labour, the punifhments of 400,000 negroes, ought to be left entirely to the difcretion of their maf-; ters; till he can affirm, that flaves have an adequate remedy, either in law, opinion, or intereft, as practifed or underftood among us, againft the parfimony, infenfibility, prejudices, meannefs, ignorance, fpite, and cruelty of their owners and overfeers; till he can fhew, that the prefent ftate of our flaves is the beft poffible ftate, both for them and their mafters, into which they can be put; and that we had a right to ravifh them from their country, to tranfport, and place them in our own; till he can fhew it to be *impoffible* to make them real Chriftians, or to render them more ufeful members of the ftate than they are at prefent; till he can fhew that reafon is convinced, humanity pleafed, that liberty has no claim, and religion no wifh; the juftice of our remarks muft remain eftablifhed, and the neceffity of that attention to the improvement of flaves, both as men and Chriftians, which is here enforced, muft remain unconfuted.

May God, in his providence, in his goodnefs, efteem us a people worthy of a bleffing, fo

valuable

valuable and extensive as the social improvement and conversion to Christianity of our
slaves would indisputably be. In this prayer,
every pious, humane, and considerate reader
will join with

The AUTHOR.

F   I   N   I   S.